IT WAS ALL JUST WORDS, REALLY, FOR FORTY YEARS— WASN'T IT?

IT WAS ALL JUST WORDS, REALLY, FOR FORTY YEARS— WASN'T IT?

Recollections of a former teacher of Communication

JUNE WEBB

iUniverse LLC
Bloomington

IT WAS ALL JUST WORDS, REALLY, FOR FORTY YEARS—WASN'T IT?
Recollections of a former teacher of Communication

iUniverse books may be ordered through booksellers or by contacting:

iUniverse LLC
1663 Liberty Drive
Bloomington, IN 47403
www.iuniverse.com
1-800-Authors (1-800-288-4677)

ISBN: 978-1-4917-2393-7 (sc)
ISBN: 978-1-4917-2391-3 (e)

Printed in the United States of America.

iUniverse rev. date: 02/04/2014

Contents

Introduction

I have attempted, with the series of recollections in this book, to share some of the flavour of my life and teaching career. The book spans a period starting with recollections of my own family's school experiences in England as far back as 1932, and continuing until my retirement in Australia in 1985. During the English 'piece' of my career, I graduated with an M.A. from Cambridge University, taught at three schools and a Technical College, got married and thus switched from being called 'Miss Richardson' to 'Mrs Webb', and had three children.

Once the family had emigrated to Australia, I embarked upon a long and very fulfilling career in lecturing at Sydney Teachers' College and Sydney University, in English, Theology, and Education—all various aspects of Communication. I wrote this book in 1995, with the intention that some of my 'Special Education' recollections, in particular, might prove interesting and useful in future.

PART I

ENGLAND

1. Early Family Life

The trouble they had, trying to communicate in Infants and Primary!

a) Alan

"Mum, why don't teachers believe what you tell them?"

"Don't they, love? What is it this time?"

"Well, Uncle Richard **does** have a car called an Oldsmobile, doesn't he? He took us kids for a ride in the dickey-seat, didn't he?"

"Yes, love, that's right. Why d'you want to know that?"

"Well, today at school our teacher asked us to tell him the names of any cars we knew, so's he could write them up on the board for spelling practice. When I said "Oldsmobile" he shouted at me not to be so silly, he wanted names of cars that exist, **not** one I'd made up. All the class laughed at me. I felt awful . . ."

"I'm sure you did, love. Come and have a cuddle! P'raps it'll make you feel better soon, to know that you were right and your teacher was wrong, this time . . . He'll feel awful when he first **sees** an Oldsmobile, won't he? Maybe we'll ask Uncle Richard to take you to school in his car, and then find an excuse to get your teacher to come outside and see him there!".

"Yes, Mum! That's a great idea! I feel better now."

"Tell you something, Alan? I'd nearly forgotten how **I** felt when my teacher didn't believe **me**! Do you remember, when you started in Kindergarten, how I told you that I went to school when I was only three? They let me begin a year early because your Grandma and Grandad were so busy in the shop. Once, I tried to tell my teacher about 'My Sisters'—I shall never forget **that** conversation!"

b)   Helen

Kindergarten teacher (1932): "How many of you have brothers and sisters?"

Helen: "**I** have **lots** of sisters, Miss Pickles, but not any brothers."

Teacher: "Oh Helen! What a tale! You **know** you have just **one** sister! She used to be in my class, so of **course** I know. Her name is Jean, she's seven years old and in Miss Doran's class, isn't she?"

Helen: "Oh no, Miss Pickles, Jean isn't my **real** sister. She keeps trying to get me to say she **is**, when we're in bed at night. But I keep telling her she's my **pretend** sister. I have lots of **real** sisters— hundreds of them—I see some of them every day. They look after me. My Canal sisters, River sisters, Wood sisters, Cloud sisters . . ."

Teacher (very patiently): "Where and when exactly do you see them, Helen?
What do they look like? Like any of us? **Do** tell us—it's News Time after all. We're all dying to hear about these imaginary sisters of yours, aren't we, children?"

Helen (weeping): "You're all laughing at me—you don't believe me!"

o-o-o-o-o-o-o-o-o-o-o-o-o-o

Alan: "Oh Mum! You felt just like me! What did you do next? Could you tell **your** Mummy about it, like me?"

Helen: "Not really . . . I did try, but **my** Mum and Dad kept telling me not to tell such stories, and to keep a check on my imagination before it got me into trouble! My big sister, your Auntie Jean, was more bothered that **she** couldn't see my other sisters, and that I insisted through thick and thin that **she** wasn't my **real** sister!"

Alan: "Didn't anybody believe you, ever?"

Helen: "Our little maid Nellie came nearest. She said she was almost sure she'd seen some of my sisters once, on the Canal bank behind our house when she was out walking with her young man."

Alan: "Could you tell **me** about them? I'd love to meet them, if I could! D'you think they'd trust me 'cos I'm yours?"

Helen: "Tell you what—I'll write it all out for you to read—it's time I made the tea now, or the girls'll be home from High School before it's ready, and then we **shall** be in trouble, shan't we? We can pretend that "Sisters" is a story for your reading practice, eh?"

So that's what they did!

0-0-0-0-0-0-0-0-0-0-0-0-0-0

c)   Charles

This seven-year-old had a special gift for working with his hands. The following episode happened at the end of an Art/Craft lesson, one in which the children had been learning about curved shapes. They had all been given sheets of bright-coloured shiny paper with circles, ovals, crescents and ellipses traced on them.

(Do you remember those red and purple and green and royal-blue shiny paper sheets from your Year 1 or 2 days? I don't think any of us was allowed cutting-out scissors while still in Kindy!).

Anyway, Charles's class had already learnt how to trace, cut out and fold the stiffer cartridge paper in order to make little boxes, and

Charles had been praised then for the sheer accuracy and detailed perfection of his tracing, cutting and folding. I wonder if he'd inherited his manual skills from his father, who was a master-printer?

Today, as he was planning so carefully to get a perfect circle out of his square of purple paper, he realised it would come out better if he cut roughly round the traced shape first. Then he could so much more easily trim neatly round the rim of his circle. It worked wonderfully! His teacher decided to get him to demonstrate in front of the whole class how he'd achieved such a great result.

Teacher: "Charles! That's really good!"

Charles: "Thankyou, Miss Brownlee. I like doing this kind of work."

Teacher: "Come out to the front, to show the other children how you did it, will you?"

Charles: "Yes, Miss Brownlee, if you want me to do that."

Teacher: "Children! All come and sit on the floor round my desk, and watch Charles. He's going to show us how he cut such a perfect circle—see it? (She held it up for the whole class to see.) Right! Here's a fresh square of coloured paper, Charles—off you go! Watch carefully, everybody!"

As he had done earlier, Charles cut quickly and roughly round the circle shape, leaving about a centimetre to be trimmed off closely in Stage 2 of the operation. As he discarded the unwanted bits of shiny purple paper, his teacher lost her temper and self-control completely.

"Charles! You stupid little boy! Didn't I ask you to show the others how beautifully you'd done your cutting? **That's** not beautiful . . . it's ugly . . . **ugly**. Why did you cut so roughly? Are you trying to be naughty deliberately? To make me look foolish in front of the class?

Well, let me tell you something—**you're** the one who's going to look foolish. Go and sit in your place. Try to mend your manners, and don't let me catch you being so smart again, or your parents will get to know about it. Do you hear?"

Did he hear? When he told me about it fifteen years later, he was still feeling hurt and humiliated that he hadn't been given a chance to explain or to demonstrate his bright idea to his teacher or to the other kids. Especially after Miss Brownlee had seemed so impressed when she saw his first **finished** effort—not having seen how he'd achieved it. "You'd think," he said, still puzzled, "that she'd have liked to know how I'd worked out for myself a different way of doing it, wouldn't you? Why do some teachers seem to think a kid's trying to outsmart them, or something, if they ever do anything different from the rest? Why do you never get a chance to talk to them, and put things right?"

o-o-o-o-o-o-o-o-o-o-o-o-o

Those three episodes in Infant and Primary school all happened to members of my own family, and as you can tell, they've stayed in the memory-banks of the clan! It was, therefore, no surprise to me to discover in 1969, when I started lecturing in English at Sydney Teachers' College (as it was then) that many of my students had similar stories to tell. More than a few of their memories of early school days focused miserably on wetting the floor, after not being believed when they told the teacher they needed to go to the toilet.

"How does **any** kid get the teacher to realise when it's genuine?"

So often they wanted an answer to that one!

"Well," says I, "how are you folks going to cope with that one yourselves, when you're on the other side of the desk?"

Which somehow brings me to remember the sorts of difficulties people have had, and have told me about, in their Secondary school days. Not to mention the ones I experienced myself, first as a pupil and then as a teacher!

Here's one of my most vivid recollections—going back to February 1938, so you can see the impression it made. My family moved house from Hebden Bridge, in Yorkshire, to Morecambe, in Lancashire. So my sister and I had to go to 'a new school'—namely Morecambe Grammar School. This is how I fared.

On the first morning, as I stood beside a kindly but unfamiliar Headmaster, I faced a silent, unknown clan. They stared blank-faced, not at all interested or welcoming. Who **was** this short, plump, bespectacled intruder, her childish look accentuated by unfashionably shingled black hair? Not at all fit for **our** class.

They couldn't know that my knees were tightly pressed together with sudden fear. The intolerable moment passed. The class let out that indrawn breath of hostile indifference as I sank down, relieved but still tense, in the seat indicated by the Head, next to a serious-looking grey-eyed girl, who regarded me calmly as the Headmaster spoke to her. "Dorothy, I know I can trust you to look after a new girl for me. See that June doesn't get lost while you all move about the school between lessons, please."

"Yes, sir". Dorothy's sigh of resignation was kept back until the classroom door closed behind his quick, soldierly figure.

At the change-of-lesson bell, Dorothy swept out with all the others into the corridor, throwing a "Come **on**, kid!" over her shoulder. By the time I'd struggled to the end of the corridor, buffeted by what seemed like the entire school travelling in the opposite direction, there was no Dorothy in sight—nor, indeed, any recognisable sign of the form to which I had so recently been assigned.

Which classroom had swallowed her and them? Was I to make myself conspicuous so soon? Panic lurched in my stomach and made the soles of my feet prickle. Could this man in overalls help? No—he was the Caretaker/Handyman. He had no idea where Form III had gone.

"We can go and look at the Timetable in the Secretary's office," he said, "and then I'll take you in to the Principal—he'll know what to do with you!".

The humiliation of having to be once again taken into the classroom by the Head, together with the embarrassed anger in Dorothy's flashing grey eyes when she was told off for letting me get lost after all, reduced me to a state of impotent misery that lightened only slowly over the ensuing months.

Why had the class taken against me with such venom? Why did that first day's coolness strengthen into such sharp antipathy? When an off-hand Dougie Long asked me at Recess "How old **are** you?", why did my answer, "Twelve . . . Thirteen in June" cause the muttered retort "What cheek"? It was many unhappy weeks later that it dawned on me, they were affronted that "such a kid" (the youngest by three months) should have been thought fit to be placed in **their** elite Form. An outsider from Yorkshire into the bargain!

It might have been different if I'd been pretty, outgoing or witty, but I was plain, socially inept, and capable only of defensive sarcasm—a talent that grew mightily with use! As the months dragged by into my fourteenth summer, things began inexplicably to improve. (Well, I found it 'inexplicable' **then**: I understand it perfectly well **now**!).

"Hey! Have you seen how high the kid can jump? We'd better put her in the House team, hadn't we?"

"June! Are you **really** going to captain the Under-Fifteens for Rounders this year? I suppose they'll **have** to pick you, since you not only got the most rounders last season, but also went and broke the school record for the longest hit of a rounders ball on Sports Day!".

And as Winter 1939 approached, one prefect even said:

"Have you played hockey before, kid? Had some coaching? You're not half bad for such a little 'un." (I ought to've remembered that when I got my Hockey Blue in my first year at Cambridge, didn't I? At least then my sport-mad tennis-champion father felt let off the hook, for all his first-born was a **daughter**!).

So, after two long years I was accepted in spite of a bad start. Even today, fifty-six fulfilling and happy years later, the memory of that First Day at the New School can be summoned very easily—not **quite** as vivid and painful as it was then, thank goodness.

My husband, on hearing the above account, asked me whether that experience might have been an early, maybe unsuspected influence that edged me towards choosing to teach English for Special Education.
Not to mention the times I was appointed to take responsibility for the Welfare of Girls! There certainly were enough of such influences! I'll tell you more of them as these Recollections of a Communicator proceed into my various adventures in High School teaching.

2. New to teaching—March High

In September 1947 I began my first teaching job at March High School for Girls, roughly fifty kms. from Cambridge, where I'd done my School Practice during my Dip.Ed. year. I was to teach English and Scripture, and help with Games and Sports coaching. My tutor at Cambridge Training College (now Hughes Hall, they tell me) who supervised my School Practice, judged that I taught English better than I taught Scripture, so it was no surprise to me to find myself having problems in Scripture classes that I didn't have in English classes. So much so that on one unhappily-remembered occasion I walked out of the room, sat for a few minutes in the cloakroom, then went to the Headmistress to tell her that I'd failed with that class, and couldn't face going back to it. She insisted that I could, should and must go back in there, in order above all to tackle the girl who'd been so defiant. So I did.

After asking Mary privately why she'd felt it necessary to challenge me so doggedly, I began to sense that once again, as so many years before in Morecambe, I was seen by these fenland girls as "the outsider from foreign parts." To quote my father's experience on first visiting his mother's home village of Bainbridge: the local lads, far from welcoming him, said "'e's a furriner, so let's chuck a brick at 'im."

Interestingly, the afore-mentioned Mary became the outstanding student in Scripture for that whole year, once we'd established a communicating relationship, she and I.

Here's another example of the lessons those girls gave me in communicating **outside** the classroom after a teaching session.

"Gillian, why did you make those rude remarks in class?"

"I'm not sure, Miss. P'raps I was trying to find out if you had it in you to send any of us out of the room."

"Why would you want to go outside? Were you bored?"

"Sort of, I s'pose . . . but I guess really I was trying to impress the rest of the girls by being smart . . . I'm sorry if I upset you, Miss."

"Gillian, do you think we could manage, between us, not to be forced to have this kind of corridor-talk again?"

"Yes, Miss, we can try, anyway, can't we?"

It wasn't only from my students that I learned how to communicate more effectively. Deeper insights into people's motives for their actions and attitudes came from quite unexpected directions—my girls' parents were in there too, teaching me all sorts of things! All of them gave me valuable experience in the job of becoming a good teacher of Communication!

Here's an instance that occurred fairly early in my first year of teaching. I'd been asked by the minister of the local Methodist church if I could take the Preparation for Membership classes, as he knew that I'd read Theology as well as English in my time at Cambridge, and had qualified to be a Lay preacher. Several of our senior girls were due to be received into Church Membership that year, including one of our brightest Sixth-formers, who was the daughter of a Society Steward of the church.

The classes had been running for four or five weeks, when Margaret missed a couple of attendances without approaching me to offer a reason for her absence. I asked her father if he thought she still wanted to become a communicant member.

"Really, Miss Richardson! How can you ask? Of **course** she does! She's **my** daughter!"

"Aren't we agreed that the Preparation classes are absolutely essential? Just to make sure our young people have been properly instructed before taking the step into full, adult membership?"

"Well—yes, of course we are! That's why we all felt so pleased and blessed when **you** came to March, so they could have a properly qualified instructor . . . But I must say her mother and I had never realised just how much homework Margaret would have to do in her H.S.C. year. If **you** knew how much, you'd understand how impossible it is for her to give up most of one evening every week to attend Membership class."

Naturally I **did** know about the amount of homework, since I was Margaret's English teacher and adviser for that year! However, her father hadn't yet finished telling me how unreasonable it was to expect his daughter to attend, when he could assure us she'd be **fully** prepared for church membership—he would **see** to it that she was.

"Thankyou, Mr. Little, for talking to me at such length—I can see everything so much more clearly now. I just didn't want you to think, as our Society Steward, that I'd accept unexplained absences without enquiry."

"I appreciate your concern, Miss Richardson, but you can rest content that my daughter will be fully prepared when the Service for Reception of New Members is held."

"Thankyou again, Mr. Little. I'll talk to Margaret myself at school tomorrow to reassure her."

So I did, and discovered that the girl would have been only too glad to get out of the house for an hour or so on one night of the week. **But** her parents kept her nose to the grindstone of study and homework, telling her they would square it with me, if I were to ask any questions. Heigh-ho! The things I learned about people, as well as about how to communicate!

o-o-o-o-o-o-o-o-o-o-o-o-o-o

One of the happiest associations I had was with the Fifth Form School Certificate class. There were one or two really tuned-in-to-English students in that group, and the essays they wrote for me were a great joy. So much so, they even had me believing that I was getting through to them some of my own enthusiasm for the subject!

One day after school, I was discussing the work of one of them, Audrey, with her friend Prudence. True to form, I was enthusing about Audrey's ability to write well.

"Whatever she decides to do when she leaves school, she **must** continue to develop that gift of hers for writing!" says I.

"Ricky!" expostulated Prue. She **doesn't have** a gift for writing. You should just **see** the time she spends every week on the work she does for you!"

"But Prue, she must have the inspiration to start with . . . some inner spark to make her even **want** to work at such length on her written assignments, whether they're for me or for anybody else!"

"What you don't seem to realise, Ricky, is how much Audrey **likes** you. She's absolutely determined to please you by giving in to you the kind of excellent work you want us to produce, and seem to believe we really can do!"

From that conversation on, I really began to understand properly the nature and importance of the human factor in teaching people anything at all. Not only English, or the art and skill of communicating effectively. I'm sure I ought to have cottoned on to that vital aspect long before, considering the succession of inspiring teachers who had brought me to where I stood, that day in 1949.

After all, it had been one of those influential people who put it to a group of us in Cambridge that unless those of us who seemed to be loving, caring types decided to become teachers, the profession would be filled with "rat-bags"!! (I must say, in our student innocence we hadn't **much** idea what rat-bags were! But it was clear they couldn't be A Good Thing, judging by the expression on our mentor's face.) So that was the decider: until that day, I'd **never** imagined myself as a teacher.

Mind you, at that point my mother reminded me that she'd always told me I'd **never** make a teacher. "You haven't the patience", she said. As for my father's reaction—well, I'll tell you. He was a pharmacist and optician, as was my mother, and he'd set his heart on seeing at least **one** of his children qualify as a doctor. (Sound familiar to anyone? Especially to any eldest daughters out there?)

Hard luck . . . his eldest child's gifts didn't lie in the area of those essential Science subjects, but in the Arts subjects of English, History and Languages. Not to be beaten in his aspirations for me, he next set his heart on my going into the Foreign Office. **Then**, he thought, I **might** become Britain's first Woman Ambassador to somewhere or other! I must say I've sometimes wondered since my arrival in Australia in 1965 whether what he imagined for me didn't happen anyway, even without the aid of the F.O. Well, of course, much had to wait until my students began to comprehend my Lancashire/Cambridge accent, and I their Australian one! I must say I've always done better at Strine than they did, but then, Languages and Lingo were my strong suit right from Morecambe Grammar school days!

Be quiet, girl. There are still lots of memories from the years between 1950 and 1964 to pass on to you, so let's proceed in proper order, eh? As they say in all the best-regulated families.

3. Unexpected Interlude—Morecambe High

As I was due to marry Norman Webb in August 1951, my parents asked me to return home to Blackpool, and maybe help in their chemist's shop. My grandmother, then aged 75, was living with us, and both she and my mother wanted my company for that last year in which I would be available. After all, it had been seven years since I'd left home to go to Cambridge, so it seemed only right and loving and filially-dutiful in a Lancashire fashion! Added to which, I was getting far too fond of and involved in the lives of my March High School girls. It was time for a change.

The change I got, though, wasn't exactly what my family and I had bargained for. The Headmaster of my old school, Morecambe Grammar, died very unexpectedly at the end of that year. (Mind you, there's a sense in which it could well have been expected, as we'd all known of the damage that had been done to his lungs in a gas attack during W.W.I.)

He had been teaching the Sixth Form Religious Education (R.E.), including those who wanted to take it as an H.S.C. subject, and Second Form Maths and Latin. The school knew that I was now living thirty or so miles away, was 'free', and especially had the necessary qualification to take H.S.C. Religious Education. **So** they telephoned Blackpool.

My father's working-class dedication to education made it impossible for him to hesitate. He regarded it as an honour that I should be asked, and by my 'old school' at that! After all, the bus journey took only an hour, and I'd still be **living** at home, wouldn't I?

Whereupon yet another of my 'learning experiences' began. The fun part of it was getting the absolutely essential help I needed every morning from the Maths master, Jimmy Ryder, and the Latin master, Taffy Owen—both of whom had been **my** teachers from 1938-43! They showed me what to teach the class, encouraged me by saying that a good teacher can teach **anything**, and checked what I'd achieved when I reported back to them. Dear people!

Apart from the usual reaction I got from the Sixth Form Scripture group, who wanted to know how I could possibly be so sure of what I was telling them on the Bible and Church History fronts, I had no arguments to worry about. As one of my March girls said once, "Miss Richardson doesn't have the usual discipline problems. She talks so fast, nobody has a chance to interrupt, or even to **think** how to stop the flow, except when she asks questions!" First of all I thought it a compliment, next a bit of a joke and finally, when I taught in an inner London school, **not true**!

4. Coventry and Sheffield—Technical Education

After my marriage in 1951, Norman and I went to live in Coventry, in the Lockhurst Lane church manse. There, among other things, we embarked on engendering our family of two girls and a boy. In 1954, the local college of Further Education wanted a part-time, one-afternoon-per-week English tutor for a class of apprentices. As our local church hall was to be rented for the purpose, it didn't seem to be too difficult for me to offer my services. So I did.

Here's the episode that's proved to be the most unforgettable, out of a term of teaching those guys. I was trying hard to make them keenly aware of the nature of Advertising, so that they wouldn't too easily part with their wages on shoddy or not-needed consumer goods. Nor be unaware of the way the world of advertising plays on a range of human emotions. So I asked each of them to bring with them the following week an example of an ad. cut from a magazine or newspaper. (Radio and T.V. to follow later!). This ad. to be one they thought to be outstandingly effective, and that they would be ready to explain why they thought so.

As I went into the room the next week, it was obvious from the general excitement that **some** of them had come up with really entertaining, hopeless, and/or teacher-challenging examples. They seemed to be glancing and grimacing slightly in the direction of one particular student—one who'd previously shown a talent for communication, so I asked for his offering soon after the lesson started.

He held up a whole-page colour ad. from a Woman's magazine. A stunning blonde model smiled at us, wearing an even more stunning white lace uplift bra. (You may be old enough to remember the time in the Fifties when "Hollywood Bosoms" were all the rage!). Not for the first time I was to be thankful for my Gemini speed of mind and tongue. The class was waiting eagerly to enjoy my discomfiture, naturally.

"My word, Dave, that's a fascinating choice you've made, isn't it, everybody?"

"**Ye-es** Miss!" "**Not half!**" came from more than one tongue.

"Now let's consider it's effectiveness as an ad. Do you suppose that picture, or the accompanying text, would persuade **any** reader to buy and wear a bra like that one?"

"Oh yes, Miss. I'm **sure** of that."

"That's really interesting, Dave. Have you bought yours yet? Do show us, won't you?"

"Well . . . no-o Miss, I haven't actually . . ."

"Oh well, I can understand that, Dave. I guess it might be too expensive to buy just to give as a present, eh? And I don't imagine you'd have much occasion to wear it yourself, would you?

Many thanks for bringing in such an interesting subject for today's discussion on the power of advertising, anyway, Dave. We shan't forget it, shall we, guys?"

0-0-0-0-0-0-0-0-0-0-0-0-0

My husband's next post was in the Carver Street Circuit in Sheffield, where we took up residence in September 1956. As luck or fate or providence would have it, the Granville College of Further Education was given an existence and a building of its own, separate from the College of Technology in Sheffield, in 1958. I was appointed there to lecture in English and History to a mixture of day-release students. Some were technical apprentices, others office trainees, all from the many steel-works of Sheffield. I had the chance to go into their work-places, to see the white-hot ingots of steel emerging from the furnaces on to the foundry floor, where they cooled to red-hot as they were rolled. That was a sight and an experience I'd **never** imagined having in my life.

Out of the five happy years I had with those day-release students, the main fruit came to ripeness when I began my period of lecturing in Communication in 1981, in Sydney. At that time, the division in which I was teaching was called Technical Teacher Education, a part of Sydney Teachers' College. Nowadays it's called the Institute of Technical and Adult Teacher Education (I.T.A.T.E.), but I believe it's still one division of Sydney College of Advanced Education. However, once again I have to remind myself that there are still many other vital memories, influences and experiences that I want to tell you about, before starting on the Australian half of this odyssey.

Come to think of it, my first morning at Granville College of F. E. proved to be quite a lesson in my **own** further education! (After all, people are always telling us that learning never stops, unless we're mentally dead, aren't they? That's moderately encouraging for times when unfamiliar experiences happen, isn't it?). As I was saying . . . after I'd reported to the Principal, Mr. George Croft, I was taken along to the Staff-room, to be introduced as the new member of the English/History/Social Studies department. I was highly intrigued to be meeting and getting to know a whole range of teachers from areas of expertise I'd never met in schools. Naturally not, since Technical and Further Education colleges don't cater for the same needs, students and courses as do High Schools, which up to then had been my only working environment.

One of the men who lectured in Automotive Engineering came across to speak to me, asking where I'd come from, and what were my qualifications for teaching Day-Release students. Had I had any previous experience in the field? Another one came over a trifle anxiously, explaining that the painted lines in the college car-park had faded during the summer break. Would I please go down there with the paintbrush and tin of paint he'd find for me, so that as my first useful job I could repaint the lines before students arrived on the following day?

I wasn't about to 'act like a girl' and refuse the job, telling those chaps that I didn't know **how** to paint lines on the bitumen! Off I went, quite unable to kneel down to do the job, as in those days women teachers were not expected or allowed to go to work in trousers! My main problem was that I couldn't persuade the brush to make a full, even line. I told Eric so, when I'd finished the job and gone back inside, **then** admitting that I'd never in my life held a paintbrush before.

"I can see you haven't", he replied. "Didn't anybody ever tell you to use the brush in **both** directions? Up as well as down?"

Fascinating, the episodes you remember most in your life-education! Not that I've **needed** to paint car-park lines since then, but if I **did**, I'd be able to, wouldn't I? Although even in the trousers I wear most of the time these days, the job might still be beyond me in my late sixties, eh?

Now for the last and most powerful of my experiences in an English school setting. All of them preparing me, I guess, for the second half of my teaching life that was to begin in January 1965.

5.   London, September 1963 to December 1964—Shelburne

Sixteen months seems such a short time to contain the definitive experiences that turned me irrevocably in the direction of a passionate involvement with Special Education. When my student teachers in Sydney during the '70s used to ask me, how come a Cambridge M.A. could possibly know or care about the problems in learning that so many children seem to have, especially in reading, and in language work generally, I told them about my London adventures. I'm pretty sure they thought I was laying it on a bit thick! Maybe you will, too!

When we finished our time in Sheffield, my husband was assigned to the job of Senior S.C.M. Secretary in London University. So we had first of all to find schools for the children, and then, naturally, one for me! I went up to town for the interview, and when I was appointed Head of Upper School at Shelburne School for Girls in Holloway, I was elated. Granted it would be my first experience of an Inner London school, but by now I truly believed there wasn't much I couldn't handle. Hadn't I just completed five years' teaching of steel-works apprentices in Yorkshire? What North Country girl would doubt that she could show these Londoners a thing or two?

Anyway, I'd applied for the job because I wanted the challenge of difficulty and Special Responsibility for Girls. (I certainly got it!) My Sheffield colleagues couldn't shake my confidence by their teasing references to the fact that "To Sir, With Love" had been written only fifteen or so years earlier, about a school very close to Shelburne. (It turned out that the parents of some of "my girls" had been there at the time!).

In September '63, when term began, I found that I'd been given an office right at the top of the three-storey building. It was to become a much-used counselling room before the year was out. I rarely left it much before six in the evening, so it became a comfortable and familiar garment. From this elevated perch I could see right across the busy, teeming district to the main road North, its traffic noise and fumes diminished by being so far below me. There were large and small depots, factories and stores; tall, plain blocks of flats; endless rows of roofs and chimneys spread hard and smoky across roads and railway lines. The whole area was crowded, commercial and cosmopolitan.

The school population was made up of English, West Indian, Greek and Turkish Cypriot and long-settled Italian families. All had widely-differing ambitions for the education of their daughters.

All of these factors inevitably gave me an abiding interest in our Migrant Education problems here in Australia. Here, as in London, family patterns of social control and expectation vary widely.

We had acute problems at times with after-school and evening activities such as Drama and Dance, especially when it came to the Annual Concert. One of our West Indian girls was very gifted as an actress, as well as being a superb dancer. Right through the school drama periods of rehearsal, her teacher grew more and more delighted by her grace, her absorption, her intensity, her ability to lift the performances of all the others.

Came the opening night, and the star didn't show up. A frantic teacher rushed round to her house, only to find an irate father, who insisted that **his** daughter was **not** going to be allowed out at night 'for some no-good reason'.

"She locked in her room. I taken away her clothes. Only **bad** girls walk the city streets at night", he said, flatly refusing to believe the story of a school concert. "No school works after seven o'clock at night! She's just trying to get out to meet men."

The Drama teacher finally managed to persuade him that she at least was speaking the truth; that he ought to come with Yvonne to the performance, and see for himself how proud he should be of his immensely talented daughter.

"I am **not** proud—I am ashamed. No decent man in our community will marry her if she makes a public exhibition of herself, showing her body on stage to everybody!"

o-o-o-o-o-o-o-o-o-o-o-o-o-o

"Madam! Quick! Can you come up to the music-room, please? There's a terrible fight going on."

So began one of the more memorable occasions I had to deal with outside my own teaching periods. Away I went at top speed, wondering who on earth could be **fighting** when there was a teacher in the room. Screams and bellowings sounded louder and louder as I tore up the stairs to the music-room. My headlong approach was blocked by three dark bodies hunched sulkily on the top step. Raising my eyebrows questioningly at them, but not slowing up more than was needed to squeeze past them, I shot into the room.

Two West Indian girls and one English girl were tearing into each other, their flailing arms and legs occasionally connecting with anyone who came close enough in an attempt to stop the fight. Just as I was about to slam a desk-lid in order to announce my presence, the fighters spotted me and heard their mates hissing "It's Madam! Lay off!"

Slowly the class of fourteen-year-olds stood up, gradually falling quiet. Expressions varied from the defiant snarls of the fighters, not yet relaxed, to the sheepish dropped eyelids of some of the onlookers. I daren't even look at the elderly Music master, ineffectually waving his hands and blustering as he tried to 'explain' what all the racket was about. I looked from one face to another, searching.

"Well, 4B, this is pretty disappointing. Beverley, can you tell me what happened?" I asked the West Indian class captain.

"He sent three girls outside for smoking, Madam, . . ."

"**HE**?" (How pompous and out-of-place it felt to be insisting on 'manners' in this setting.)

"Yes, Madam, Mr. Smith did, and . . ."

"Do you mean they were smoking in **class**, Beverley?"

"No, Madam. They went down to the toilets, but you could smell the smoke about them when they came back. **Then** he said . . ."

"It wasn't just that," cut in Smithy. "They were so cheeky when they came back—laughing as if they'd done something clever. It was not to be borne!—These West Indians don't know how to behave! **Especially** after I gave them permission to leave the room in good faith—it's insulting to have my kindness treated as if it were weakness. **That's** what upset me the most."

"He never sends white girls out, whatever they do!" erupted from another dark girl, near to tears. "Everybody's against us in this place, but we're as good as any of you, just you see if we aren't!"

"Hang on just a sec.," I intervened. "Why those who were **not** sent out felt they had to fight each other isn't yet clear to me, but come back to my office with me, so's we can discuss the whole thing. I'm sorry your class has been upset, Mr. Smith. I'm sure you'll be able to get on better now."

I emerged from the room, trailing six young adults for a cooling-off period in my office, realising that they needed to be taken out from under the harrow just as much as Smithy needed a respite from the problems they set him.

o-o-o-o-o-o-o-o-o-o-o-o-o-o

Whereas the above episode taught me a lesson in one kind of migrant problem, mixed with teacher-pupil relationships, this next one gave me some very different, equally valuable insights.

"Madam, may I bring my parents in to see you? They would like to talk to you about some special problems I've been having."

This one was a complete surprise. The girl was one of our most promising H.S.C. students, nearly nineteen and a rare charmer. She was a Turkish Cypriot who had learned English well enough to be able to interpret for me when we had non-English-speaking parents in to see us about their daughters' problems.

Remember that this was in 1964, when the situation in Cyprus was so bad that many refugees, both Greek and Turkish, had fled to London. This particular Sixth-Form girl was the leader of the Turkish girls in the school, and was usually noticeably bright and happy. Not at this time though, as was immediately obvious when she ushered her mother and father into my room. It was to become clear very rapidly that the difficulty lay in the fact that Nedjla **was** the leader of the Turkish Cypriot girls.

After the proper polite preliminaries, her father said slowly, "We do so want Nedjla to do well in her exams, so's she can become a doctor or a lawyer. Then she could serve our people in the hard years ahead. Not **fight**."

My encouraging smile must have started to look a bit puzzled at this point. Why on earth **should** the girl have to consider fighting in her future at all? Her father tried to explain more clearly why they'd come for help, by saying "Nedjla cannot study well because of the fighting. The fighting **here** at the **school**."

With help from Nedjla, light began to dawn. The Greek Cypriot girls outnumbered the Turkish girls, with the result that teasing, taunting and pushing around were getting stronger and heavier in the playground. Both factions had taken to asking their brothers to come round from the neighbouring boys' school during the lunch-hour, and some of the girls were themselves carrying knives. One girl had fallen down a flight of steps in the yard when threatened by a group with a knife. Things were getting very serious indeed. How come we hadn't noticed it for ourselves?

As leader of the smaller group, Nedjla was beginning to feel herself unable to defend Turkish Honour. The responsibility was too great, and **now** the fear of possible bloodshed was making her school-work suffer.

The wonder to me was how any of them could **ever** give their minds to 'school-work', being forced as they were to reflect the troubles of their homeland.

I reassured Nedjla's parents that I would make sure the Staff knew what was going on. I'd ask for their co-operation when they were on playground supervision duty so that we didn't accept reported 'accidents' too easily. And if at any time Nedjla was in need of comforting, counselling or help with her academic work, she could come to talk to me.

That's how I learned more about race-relations, and the problems they can cause in schools as well as in the wider community.

o-o-o-o-o-o-o-o-o-o-o-o-o

I must admit that the next 'recollection' of my time in London probably turned out to be the most powerful influence of all on the path towards Special Education. Tell you why.

It had been wisely decided that I ought to get to know the most difficult classes as soon as possible, so that my role as counsellor, with special responsibility for the welfare of the girls, would be more logically workable and useful. My teaching time had to be limited to allow for such counselling, and also for my administrative duties as Head of Upper School. That meant that my first teaching subject, English, requiring at least five periods per class per week, couldn't serve for 'getting to know you' in every one of our difficult classes. So my second method subject, Religious Education, needing only one or two periods a week with each class, was therefore decided upon.

The only drawback to **that** course, as I was soon to find out, was the universal antipathy in the school to "Scripture".

The most jolting lesson I was ever to receive in my life as a teacher started on my second day at Shelburne. It had been hard enough for me to be addressed as 'Madam', after all those years of being called 'Miss'—(to my face, at least!). However, I managed to accept that Londoners were accustomed to address their female teachers as Madam, no brothel-keeping implied.

I went into my Fourth Form (Year 9) class, intending, as I always did with new groups, to find out what they'd already covered of the Syllabus, and which of the remaining alternatives they'd most like to tackle next. That way we might both enjoy the lessons.

There was an air of steady preoccupation over the room. Girls were talking nineteen to the dozen, some sitting with their backs to the door, others propped on their elbows, leaning towards their friends. A few reading magazines, or knitting. They stood up to answer my greeting, all animation gone from their faces. Then, they dropped back into their seats, momentarily still. Waiting.

Time to establish a relationship, June. No way out now.

"So that we don't do the same old things and get bored, I want you to tell me please what parts of the book your previous teacher did with you last year . . ."

I didn't get any further.

"D'you go up West again last night, Shirl?" shouted one girl in the front row to another at the back.
It was the signal for everybody to resume her prior occupation.
Just as in the Awakening scene in "Sleeping Beauty", animation returned.
Instantly, the girls in the back row who'd been fixing false eyelashes whipped out their mirrors and kits. Friends moved over to look, comment, hold the mirrors for them. Others resumed brushing, back-combing and spraying their bee-hive hair-dos, while the rest continued their conversations from the point at which my untimely arrival had so rudely interrupted them.

Stunned, I thought incredulously "This sort of thing happened in 'To Sir, With Love'—and a faraway tinkle of sardonic Northern laughter came through the hubbub.

The girls in the front row nearest to me waited for a long moment, watching to see what I'd do.
I tried asking **them** what I needed to know, as if my dazed wits might return if I gave them time, and acted as if nothing out of the ordinary was happening. I've wondered since how many teachers do this all the time. The class 'captain', embarrassed for me, plied me with 'good advice':

"**Shout** at them, Madam, real loud. That's all they'll take notice of. It's what we're used to, see, here **and** at home. We only learn the real hard way, kids like us. **Go on, Madam, SHOUT!**"

Shout at them? But they were people, surely? I wouldn't shout at an adult: why then should I shout at adolescents? I'd never had to raise my voice in class in sixteen years of teaching; I wasn't going to start now.

I stood there, frantically trying to recall the class-control methods of all the good teachers I'd ever had, while feeling nightmare-doomed. None of them had stood in front of a class that so single-mindedly went about its own concerns, apparently regarding the teacher as not present, or at any rate not relevant.

For several weary weeks I plugged along, trying 'interesting' approaches, getting one or two to speak to me individually, putting arresting drawings, posters, captions on the board. Waiting, trusting and hoping for a whole-class response. Every time the racket of talk and laughter went on as before.

"They're trying you out," I told myself. "Stick it out. Never forget they've got years of resentment to work off. Don't give in and yell, or they prove their point, don't they?"

One day when I went in, a girl from the back row was standing by my desk.

"Look, Madam," she began in a confidential tone. "You get yourself something to do, eh, and don't bother us; we'll keep fairly quiet, doing what **we** like—that's talk to one another. How about it, eh?"

Don't think I wasn't tempted!

She went on: "Nobody's taught us anything useful at all since we first came to this school. We're all just waiting the time out 'til we're old enough to leave school—so you're only banging your head against a wall, trying to teach us Scripture, really, aren't you Madam?"

Familiar? Insulting? Not intentionally, I realised. Just honest, forthright, and above all astonishingly **friendly**. I grasped quickly at what was to my mind a proffered straw; a possible way through!

"There must be some topics we could **all** discuss, surely? What if we look for some things to talk about together that you **would** enjoy?"

Her retort came London-quick.

"**You** wouldn't want to talk about what **we're** interested in!"

Guffaws all round.

"Why not? Do you all suppose I haven't 'lived' at all? **I've** got three kids of my own, you know—how d'you imagine **they** arrived? By way of the stork; in the doctor's little black bag? Life's the same for everybody, isn't it?"

"Not it! It's different for us and you by a long way! Come on, Madam, you must be joking!"

"Look! If you don't believe me now, I'll tell you what we could do. You all write down on slips of paper the things you **really** want to talk about. We'll put them in a box: the class captain can pick them out with her eyes closed, and I promise you we'll discuss them in whatever order they come out of the box. You don't have to put your names on the paper, either!"

They decided to try it, on the ground that it sounded less awful and useless than any more of the fare they'd been offered up to that point.

That was the beginning of real understanding and communication with that class. Naturally some of them went on reading their 'True Confessions' magazines, whatever the topic picked out of the box might be, but most of them asked for what they really wanted to know, as we tackled such vital issues and life-situations as we could think up between us. Here's a list of a few of them:

Parents and Children—shall I think **I** know it all when I'm my parents' age? Will **my** kids think I'm as wrong about them as I know Mum and Dad are about me?

Boyfriends—why does my boyfriend call me a slag? I've told him a girl can tear her hymen by falling across a fence, as I did. That's true, isn't it?

Morality, Religion and Sects—why can't you find out from experience what's right and what's wrong, without people telling you "It is because God says so"?

Ghosts—I'm sure I'm not the only one in this class who's seen and felt the presence of Spirits. Why can't we talk about such experiences seriously, instead of always being teased and put down, as if we're stupid?

I'll put down the others more briefly, or I shall find myself writing out the whole discussion we had on each topic!

Relationships in the work-place; Why school is so irrelevant, and what 'They' ought to teach you instead; Epic Biblical films and their relationship to the original story; Abortion, V.D. and the future of the family.

My proudest moment came on the day they said wonderingly "Nothing we can ask you shocks you, does it, Madam?"

Many of them left school the day they turned fifteen, so the early size and strength of the opposition in that class died away without ever being properly won over. I'm sure they'll never know how completely they won **me** over! Looking at one 'problem child', Teresa, one day, I had to acknowledge how right they'd been when they insisted that "Life **isn't** the same for all of us."

Teresa had been moved to Shelburne after the birth of her son. The Inner London Education Authority had thought it better for her not to return to her previous school, where all her class-mates knew of her pregnancy. At a new school, she might be able to keep it a secret. I well remember the Staff Meeting after we'd been notified of her transfer to us, and the reason for it.

My colleagues wore such serious, concerned expressions that a fourteen-year-old should be in such a predicament, while **still** being too young to leave school legally. How could she possibly be expected to study or to do homework? Was she still breast-feeding?

We assured one another that we would be **most** considerate of her feelings. No mention would ever be made of her unmarried mother status. No acknowledgment or questioning of any kind would be allowed to betray the fact that we knew why she'd had to change schools. We were so shocked, bourgeois, caring and maternal!

On Teresa's first day with us, at Recess time, I heard her being made welcome by a group of curious girls. She responded by asking them enthusiastically whether they would really like to know what having a baby was like.

So much for our middle-class attitudes!

We found out later, when she felt in need of my counsel, and trusted me enough to come to my office, that the boyfriend had moved into the family's tenement flat. Teresa was keeping house for her grandfather and father, brother, boyfriend and newborn son, as her grandmother was too sick to help, and her mother had left home in despair. No, my life at any age hadn't been a bit like hers, much less at the tender age of fourteen.

Vivien was another member of the group who had had problems. Hers were somewhat different from Teresa's, in that the outcome was not the same. She came to talk to me on more than one occasion after that Fourth Form and I had got on better terms with each other.

One afternoon at the end of school she arrived at my office, asking if I had the time to deal with a worry she'd had for a week or two. I settled to listen.

"I've been going out with this boy for over six months now. Everybody who knows us both said we'd sleep together before long. Of course we did—and now I've got V.D. What's bothering me is having to go to the V.D. Clinic."

I must have looked puzzled at this, because she hurried on to add: "No, no! It's not that I'm ashamed of having to go, if that's what you're thinking. It's looking at all the others who have to go there—awful, grotty-looking old women. It was terrible to find I was the only one there under sixteen. I can't bear to look at those others, or even be in the same room with them. Do I **have** to? Is there **nowhere** else I could go to be cured?"

What could I do but let her pour it all out, encourage her to believe she **would** be cured, and strengthen her self-esteem in any possible way? "Life is the same for all of us"?
She left school at the end of the year, but I can still see her sitting dejectedly by me, hoping desperately for something good to happen in her life. And we expected homework from girls like Teresa and Vivien?

For all the hard work, staffing problems and heartache of those sixteen months at Shelburne, I really didn't want to leave in December 1964, just as I felt to be getting somewhere! I'd learnt so much about young people, and about teaching them, that I'd never known before, and although I hoped it would all come in useful in my later teaching career (it did!) I still felt sad to leave 'my girls'.

Nevertheless, when I told them at the final assembly before Christmas that my husband had been appointed to a post in Australia, they kindly agreed that perhaps I ought not to let him go on his own, men being as helpless as they were! They gave me permission to depart.

My mind goes back to the time I telephoned my father, when I was having such a shattering time at the beginning of my work in London. After I described what I was up against, he said: "Junie—are **you** going to win, or are they?" I knew very well what I was expected to say, so of course I obliged. "I am!" I said, like a dutiful daughter.

Not so, as you can tell. **You** won, dear Shelburnians, and I couldn't be more pleased that it was so.

END OF ENGLISH HALF OF MY LIFE

PART II

THE AUSTRALIAN HALF OF MY TEACHING LIFE

6. Voyage to Australia

The job my husband had been appointed to do was to take charge in February 1965 of a residential college in the grounds of Sydney University. It was to be our abode for twelve years.

As we travelled to Southampton on December 22, 1964, we felt the usual mixture of emotions. Excitement at the thought of moving to another country to work, perhaps for the rest of our lives. Sadness at leaving grandparents, friends, familiar places and influences. A heightening of nervous anticipation at the idea of going to an unknown place, where there were no friends or acquaintances as yet, no family, and certainly no familiar places.

Meantime there would be three weeks of life aboard S.S. "Oriana", another experience we'd never had before.—Among other things, I'd never **seen** a shower in my life. I **did** wish there'd been somebody around to tell me that you don't have to stand completely under the shower-head so that you can't open your eyes! It made finding the whereabouts of soap and face-washer so difficult! I'm not sure which was worse—learning to cope with showering without instruction, or having no idea **what** to do with a bidet. Just badly-brought-up, that's all!

We arrived in Naples on Christmas Eve. While the ship was in port there we were able to visit Pompeii. Here I found the remaining inscriptions and murals more than sufficiently evocative of a life about which our Latin teacher had told us twenty-five years earlier. My always-fertile imagination was stimulated even more than it had been when, in those Morecambe Grammar School days, Mr. Owen took us on an excursion to Housesteads on Hadrian's Wall!

My brother and his family had travelled out to New Zealand earlier that year. They had taken an unforgettable trip into the mountains from Colombo to Kandy. They urged us strongly to hire a taxi and do the same. Apart from some problems with motion-sickness in the bumpy old car, we found the trip memorable for lots of reasons. Our small son was lifted up onto the back of an elephant. Small children held out their hands for money wherever we went. We bought a carved teak model of an elephant and one of a stork, which we still have.

Into the bargain, I discovered that I'm hopeless as a tourist and sight-seer. I felt it was so rude to stare at people who were following their own occupations, just because they looked so different from what we were used to seeing. Even after being assured that the tourist trade was what brought in their living, I still felt unhappy to feel that they were being made into some sort of a peepshow. It strikes me today that I might have been reacting in that way because of the conditioning I'd had, fighting for my dark-skinned girls at Shelburne, and the prejudice **they'd** had to face. Possible?

Before we get to Australia I'd like to tell you about a couple of interesting people we met on board "Oriana". One was coming out from England much as we were, to take up a post as Principal of a private school. He had had experience in a Public School in England, and was regarded by the governors of the Australian school as a find, well able to run a similar establishment in a different country.
We looked forward to seeing how he got on when term began in February.

He found Australian attitudes and expectations of school to be very different from his own, and from those of his educational background in England. He had really understood that the governors had brought him out to effect 'improvements' in the running of the school. When the changes that he'd supposed he'd been engaged to make conflicted with local aspirations and parental ambitions for their sons, he became so frustrated and unhappy that he returned to work in an English Public School.

Another passenger was coming out to a University post. He had less intention of making changes than of learning what teaching style would best communicate with an Australian academic staff and student body. He had a certain advantage in being of non-English stock, although he'd lived and studied in England for the previous twenty years. Hence his success in being appointed to a top-notch Uni. post. Things went much better for him than they did for the afore-mentioned school principal, and he settled down well.

There were other passengers who were coming out to work, and some who were returning home after getting work-experience overseas: a custom we discovered to be a highly-Australian thing to do!

When the ship reached Fremantle we were met by our opposite number there, who had charge of a residential college in Perth University. He invited us to have afternoon tea at his residence, then took us to see the grounds of the University. It was January 10, and Perth was experiencing the third (or was it the tenth? It was a record, anyway, I **do** remember that!) day of over 100 degrees F.

Having left England when the temperature was nearer to 10 degrees, we were suitably stunned—and could **only** hope that Sydney didn't carry on in the same outlandish fashion! It made our first taste of China tea almost enjoyable!

My husband and I were used to being the ones who never got burnt by the sun, as we both tanned easily. So much so that I still remember being most upset and offended in the summer of 1939, when I returned to school after attending a Girl Guide camp. "**You're** a half-caste, I can see that for myself", said a class-mate. Why did that strike me as such an insult, then? Why didn't **I** think, as Dad said, "Well, since it isn't true, why not take it as a compliment to your tan?"

Mind you, nobody here in Australia needs to be told that the sun we used to get in Lancashire, Yorkshire, East Anglia or the Midlands could hardly be compared with the Australian sun! Did anybody else who's reading this get caught? It'd been degrading enough for me to get sunburnt so badly on board "Oriana", but once in Australia . . . . !

I've simply had to learn to keep out of what I'd always imagined to be my native element, born as I was on a hot June day in Burnley. (My mother told me that the midwife had said: "If there'd bin a barber in t' street a'd've 'ad me 'ead shaved!")

Still, all the heat on that day of our arrival didn't stop us from finding the Park in Perth amazingly beautiful. The next day, when the ship called at Melbourne, it was raining too much for us to see anything much of the city. We had to do that on other occasions, when we were there for conference and later for a Drama School.

7. January 12, 1965—Arrival in Sydney

We reached Sydney, and I was the only member of the family not to see that magical view of the harbour as "Oriana" came in through the Heads. It fell to me as a 'migrant mother' to queue up inside, in order to be interviewed by Immigration Officers and Department of Education officials who had come on board to check the passengers and their reasons for coming to Australia.

One member of our family, a foster-daughter, was a Primary School teacher. She had had much the same kind of experience, teaching in an inner London school as I had had at Shelburne. In her case, however, the physical roughness at Primary level had resulted in her being severely kicked in the shins—an injury that needed hospitalisation in Sydney when thrombosis developed. That didn't happen for quite a few months, thank goodness, and it cleared up before too long.

However, being assigned to a school in the first place wasn't simple. We'd enquired of Australia House when we knew we were moving from London, and had been assured there'd be "no problem", as they say in these parts! As it turned out, there certainly **were** problems for her. What was offered by the Department of Education here was a post at a school a fair distance from the Sydney Uni. campus. When asked for something a bit closer for such a newcomer to reach, Ann got told "That isn't far, as Australian distances go. Most teachers in the city travel at least that far to work. Anyway, there's a bus", they said.

"Couldn't I walk?" Ann asked. "I get bus-sick".

"Bad Luck!" was the reply. "Do you want a job or don't you, whingeing Pom?"

In the end, after a period during which my husband drove her to school and back every day, somebody in the Department must have realised how good a teacher she was. She was offered a transfer to Camperdown Demonstration School, much nearer home and making lots more use of her skills. From there she eventually moved into the Education Department of Sydney Teachers' College.

Once we had taken up residence in Wesley College at the beginning of February, insights into a different Education system came rapidly. First of all, before I began to look for work for myself, the most important consideration was how best to support the children as they tackled the job of settling into a new school in a new country. Our elder daughter took some necessary tests to find out which High School she was to attend. It turned out to be Fort Street Girls', situated in those days beside the Bradfield Expressway. (The buildings are now the S.H. Ervin gallery.)

For the two younger children the local school was Camperdown Public, to which we used to walk together each school day. I discovered there an institution quite new to me—'the Oslo'. School canteens I **had** met before, of course, and in my own high school days in Morecambe had eaten school lunches from one. Not sandwiches though. Full cooked 'School Dinner', served and eaten at tables in the school dining-room, and costing a shilling a day.

I was sufficiently intrigued by the Oslo at Camperdown to stay most mornings for a term or two to help prepare the lunches. It seemed like the proper thing for a newly-arrived migrant mother to do! And it gave the children a feeling that I wasn't so far away for a time. What's more, it was a highly enlightening period for me, showing me lots about how the System ran, and how parents talked about things among themselves. Naturally I didn't tell them anything about the job I'd been doing immediately before leaving England, nor much about the one we'd come to Sydney to do.

I was still possessed by that concern for students' learning problems, and what seemed like the inability of schools to solve them. My girls at Shelburne had influenced **my** life much more than they could have known or believed. I've hoped ever since those days that I might have made at least half as much difference to theirs.

I wanted to know what sort of provision was made in Australia to cope with such school-learning problems, so I went in to ask the Principal of Camperdown. He was very helpful, giving me copies of the relevant documents and directives from the Department of Special Education, and also those concerned with Migrant Language Education. They gave me lots of information and ideas.

As he handed them to me, 'Mr. Mac' observed: "Every Pommie teacher I meet here wants to know about Special Education. You Poms must have an awful lot of Slow Learners and backward kids in your schools! We don't have any here, you know, but still . . . if that's what grabs you!"

Back to the question of "Is it the kids or the teachers who have the problems with in-school slow learning?" How can a teacher be expected to cope with a backward or slower learner? Unless, of course the teacher has a special gift for it, or has had special training and experience. For most of us, though, it's because we were ourselves particularly bright at school that we passed the necessary exams to get into the teaching field in the first place, isn't it? For some perfectly understandable reason, therefore, many teachers in my experience feel threatened by pupils who can't seem to learn, or who can't concentrate for long enough to grasp a point.

"Listen, you lot! I've taught you this lesson **three** times already, and you **still** don't know it. What's the matter with you? Are you being deliberately stupid, or were you just born that way?"

I've heard versions of that inspiring address to the troops so often, first as a school-kid, then as a staff-member, then while supervising School Practice in later years. I'd dearly love to know how anyone can imagine that he or she has "taught a lesson", whether three times or more, if the kids haven't understood, grasped or learnt it. Would our fore-fathers have been satisfied to demonstrate only their trade, farming, home-making skills to their children, then to call them stupid if they couldn't instantly perform such tasks as well as the one who was teaching them?

After we'd settled in as a family, I went along to Sydney Teachers' College to ask if my teaching experience so far might be found useful in the training of student teachers. I was beginning to feel overloaded with 'learning experiences', so it occurred to me that I might have a contribution to offer to up-coming teachers of the future.

"But you've never even taught in Australia!" exclaimed the College Principal. "You could hardly prepare our students for an environment you haven't experienced yourself, could you?"

That's funny—I'd always been told by my own college tutors that a good teacher can teach anything, provided he or she understands the process of Teaching/Learning—how you can't have one without the other. Not to mention knowing how and where to find the subject-matter that's required, if it didn't happen to be what that teacher was trained to do in the first place! (Echoes from that time I told you about, when in 1950 I had to take on Latin and Maths at Morecambe Grammar School, and couldn't have done it without the help of the staff who'd been trained in those disciplines!)

I must say I was highly encouraged when friends and colleagues in Australia told me of how they too had been expected to 'fill in' regardless. The legends I heard! Perhaps my favourite ones were of male teachers who were put in charge of Needlework or Cookery, and female ones who had their time-tables 'filled up' with a period in the Woodwork room, or ostensibly coaching the football team.

Goodness! I wonder if the Education Department was **really** an Equal Opportunity Employer so many years before it became not only the In Thing, but also a legal requirement?

By halfway through 1965 a couple of interesting things came my way. High time I finished the story of this transition period, and started a new section. Here goes.

8. English Tutor and Scripture Educator

Naturally enough, it had become known around the University that a couple of Cambridge M.A.'s had taken up residence at Wesley College. We had been made more than welcome by the community; invited out to meals; taken to see the beauties of the Sydney area and the Blue Mountains; asked to speak at all kinds of function. Altogether overwhelmed by kindness.

At one of the University get-togethers I met Sam Goldberg, at that time the Professor of English at Sydney. He enquired whether F. R. Leavis had been lecturing in the English Department during my time at Cambridge. He had. It turned out that one or two young lecturers had recently come out to Sydney after graduating from Cambridge, at a time when interest in Leavis's theories, books and teaching were at an all-time high. Professor Goldberg asked me if I would consider taking on a job as a part-time tutor for six hours a week, as a vacancy in English I was likely to arise. I didn't exactly have to consider! I was delighted to be given the chance to teach students at a Tertiary level.

As it turned out, the number of hours needed was eight per week, so that was my commitment during term-time for the next three years. To nobody's surprise I was utterly happy doing it. The tutorial groups were moved about in the course of University building, including the construction of Fisher Library. For quite a time, several of us held our classes down under the Stacks, and although the rooms were air-conditioned, some students occasionally felt to be trapped or suffocating. At the beginning of each term I used to take all the members of my classes who were claustrophobic along to the end of that downstairs corridor. There, a door opened to the fresh air outside, and to a great view across Victoria Park into the bargain.

What's more, it was always understood between us that if they needed that kind of a break, they were to take it for granted that I was on side, just as I was if they needed to go to the toilet.

I had some absolutely brilliant students among those in my tutorial groups. I've kept a keen eye out ever since, expecting to see their names in print! So one of my big shock/surprises came at the end-of-year exam., when it was explained to us, as markers, that we must produce a certain proportion **only** of Distinction and Credit grades. The remaining candidates were to be awarded Pass, Repeat or Fail.

"There's a limit on the number of students who can be offered places in English II, so ask yourself when in doubt as to what mark to give: 'Would I want to teach this one in Second Year? Is he/she good enough to succeed? To bring credit to the Department?' That should enable you to assess the appropriate grade."

Silly me! There I was, still supposing that there was some kind of objective criterion to use when marking. In some years there were many more student essays and examination answers worthy of high marks than there were in others. How could one possibly give exactly the same proportion of Distinctions and Credits in every year, regardless of the standard of the candidature? However rationally argued the case might be.

My most notable faux-pas happened when it became clear to me that one or two of my colleagues were having trouble communicating with their tutorial-group students. For a week or two my class was enlarged by some who asked "Can I just sit in with you? I haven't managed to grasp the topic yet." As most of the tutors were exceptionally bright post-graduates who were studying for higher degrees, it stood to reason that they might well have problems in explaining to the less bright such aspects of English Literature as had always been perfectly clear to a first-class graduate.

I heard it for myself on one occasion. We'd opened our door to the corridor, so as not to feel shut in and cramped. In a small space of time, a pause in our discussion for everybody to have a think, came very loud and clear from the next room an exasperated, weary voice. "Well!" he said. "Since you don't seem to be able to answer **that** question, we shall have to try another one!"

It therefore occurred to me that there was a service I **could** render to the Department, in the light of my teaching experience up to then. I offered to take a Tutorial Staff Seminar for a week or two, or for longer if such tutors as wished to attend found it helpful to continue. I wanted simply to give them some tips on making oneself understood; on running a fruitful discussion; on asking leading questions; on reading facial expressions and body language, to be able to sense where lay any misunderstandings in the minds of class-members.

My offer was summarily rejected as being totally arrogant. How could I possibly imagine **I** had anything to offer to such clever post-graduates? Their style and method of tutoring were perfect ways to separate the wheat from the chaff. The poorer students would be weeded out that much earlier if tutorials were made really difficult! Only **true** scholars would be able to jump over all those hurdles, giving the Department an elite group to go on to later years of the Degree. Maybe to go on to become Masters of Arts and Doctors of Philosophy.

Oh, and would I please not accept into my classes any students who hadn't been written down on my list? It was much too confusing for the Record-keepers.

Once again, I lived and learned!

The other interesting thing that came my way in the same year was to be asked to lecture in the Clergy Course, run by Sydney Teachers' College in those days. It was run on one afternoon a week for one term each year, with the purpose of enabling those who taught Scripture in schools, whether clergy or lay-people, to teach more confidently and effectively. Once again the Theology component of my Degree qualifications was to prove useful.

I was asked if I could lecture especially on how to teach by means of Discussion. After my experience at Shelburne, I thought perhaps I just might be able to do that! From one of my lectures, one particular question stays in my memory, seemingly ineradicably.

"When you offer a class the chance to discuss all these vital issues, such as the nature of sin and salvation, what if they come to the wrong conclusions? Surely you couldn't allow that to happen?"

"How could you possibly teach by means of open discussion, giving your class **full** permission to speak of what's in their minds and hearts, and then tell them that they're wrong? Don't you expect to be so convincing, so well able to match **any** argument they could put forward, that the right conclusion would be sure to be reached in the end?"

"Oh no! If you only knew how contrary children are these days! I can see I'd **never** have the confidence to try to teach by means of discussion. I'll stay with the old method of just **telling** them what's right and what's wrong. How else are we going to fulfil our mission of bringing them to Jesus?"

"Surely **instructing** children is what we're required to do in our schools, isn't it?"

At this point I needed reassuring that I hadn't totally misunderstood what Scripture-teaching in schools in Australia was meant to be. So I turned to the rest of the group.

"How many of you would feel it presumptuous to have it thought that our job is to convert the children we teach, just because we've the privilege of access to them for one period a week? Preaching and Teaching aren't the same thing, in your opinion, are they?"

It seems funny now to remember how disappointed I'd been to find that Religious Education wasn't a subject taught by professionals as part of their teaching load as it had been in England. 'You won't have a chance to use your Dip. Ed. qualifications in R. E. in Australia, you know, June!' my English colleagues told me. Haha! They were wrong, and so was I to be cast down about it. That very component was to be called upon again during the following year, as I'll tell you about presently. It came about in a fascinatingly providential way.

The Head of the Education Department at Sydney Teachers' College was an outstanding person. She had graduated brilliantly in Philosophy, and whatever subjects or courses she took after that, she gained first-class results. When she decided that the time had come for her to write a book on the Philosophy of Education for students in the Faculty to use, she took a term's Study Leave in order to complete it.

In those days, lecturing and tutoring in Education was shared between the University of Sydney's department of Education and that of Sydney Teachers' College. We also offered to our trainee teachers various options in their courses, both to broaden their personal cultural knowledge and horizons, and to enable them to be better sources of such knowledge for their future pupils.

Dr. Hogg asked me therefore if I would take on both her tutorial groups in Education and her option, which was Comparative Religion. It gave me great pleasure and satisfaction to do both. In my own Degree studies of Theology, my best results were in Church History and New Testament Greek: no surprise to anyone who knew that my H.S.C. distinctions and scholarship-winning had been English, History, French and German! I was always going to be a language person, a.k.a. 'communicator', wasn't I? (No wonder my father imagined me in the Foreign Office, until I 'let the side down' by transferring from English to Theology in my third year!)

We **had** done one course of lectures at Cambridge in Comparative Religion, but I learned much more from the papers presented and discussed by those S.T.C. students, after they and I had done the required readings. Islam; Buddhism; Taoism; Animism; Spiritism and Spiritualism. And of course as many of the sects of Christianity as proved relevant to our discussions of other Faiths. Really, as so often before, I gathered so much from my students that the wicked thought occurs to me: shouldn't students be paid, or somehow rewarded, for the quantity of education they give to their teachers?! My Primary school headmaster used to give pieces of Toblerone to the children in his Sixth class who got all their sums right . . . though I hardly think chocolate would be the answer for our Secondary and Tertiary students, eh? But

45

surely we ought to be able to think of **some** reward, besides assuring them that what we're doing for them will get them a good job, and that they're privileged to be in our company, getting the benefit of our inestimable wisdom, knowledge and experience?

Will you talk sense, June?

9. S.T.C. Correspondence Courses

Being given the opportunity to stand in for Dr. Hogg wasn't the only unexpected call from S.T.C. in 1966. One of the unusual jobs the College had undertaken for many years was to write and administer Correspondence Courses for the Child Welfare Department, the Aborigines' Welfare Department, and the Housing Commission. When officers in these bodies were appointed, they were enrolled in our courses. They were informed that they would not only be better able to do their jobs, by understanding their clients' needs more clearly, they would also qualify for a permanent position and promotion.

The man who had been the lecturer in charge of Correspondence Courses became very sick towards the end of 1965. He had, therefore, been unable to mark the examination papers that had been set, done and sent in by the students on the three courses involved. Now it was February 1966, and time for a new year's work to be started. The Principal, knowing by now something of my work and availability, sent for me to ask if I could oblige him by marking those papers, and help out by doing the Correspondence work until the proper lecturer regained his health and returned to work. I could and did, being enrolled in February '66 as a Temporary Lecturer, with the enthralling Ed. Dept. number 6661912.

This turned out to be another fascinating job, giving me all sorts of insights into Australian society. I visited the Children's Court, to see for myself the kind of kid that was sent to institutions such as Yasmar, Minda, Mount Penang. Since the officers of those places were the students whose work I was to mark, I wanted to tune in to the human nature problems facing them.

It seemed possible that the units on Child Psychology and Children's Behaviour Difficulties might well have been highly useful information for a trainee teacher, while not being usable at all in a Remand Home setting. As one of the most honest of those Child Welfare officers said to me: "We realise that we **have** to put down in our answers to you all that stuff about treating the boys with understanding and compassion. Just the same, we notice that the ones who get promoted are the toughest guys, most of them ex-Army men. They all did the College course, naturally, 'cos they knew they wouldn't be promoted if they didn't, but they still believe in treating the lads harshly. One who's always held up as an example to new recruits to the Department has a special punishment for any kid he thinks is rude, not respectful enough or misbehaving on parade. He makes 'em scrub a square yard of the parade-ground with a tooth-brush! Would you call that Applied Psychology, as my old dad used to say when he belted us with his razor-strop?"

I learnt nearly as much about the ways of the Housing Commission, and through contact with the Aborigines' Welfare officers I ended up fostering a part-Aboriginal twin brother and sister for a couple of years from 1967-69. They went to school with my kids, and were a part of the family until I had to go into Gloucester House for the first of three operations on my arthritic hips. I felt a proper failure, having to let the twins go to two other foster-homes after most of the difficulties of settling in with us had been overcome.

Perhaps the most fun the Correspondence Courses provided came twice a year when we organised the face-to-face sessions at the Coogee Bay Hotel. We gave lectures on the topics the officers had to write about, then had open discussions, small-group tutorials, and question-and-answer periods. For all of us it was great to see the faces behind the written answers and markers' comments! They could so much more easily **tell** me about their jobs, their problems with writing assignments so many years after leaving school—"I was never any good at reading and writing, anyway!"—together with quite specific problems that some of them had. For example, one of the Aborigines' Welfare officers wanted to know how he could possibly function as an agent of help psychologically, when one of his jobs was to collect rents from the people supposedly in his care.

Yet another of that multiplicity of life-learning-experiences I had, adding to the pressure towards lecturing in Special Education.

Even though I never **did** teach officially in an Australian school, I stayed with the College in sundry capacities until my retirement in 1985. The lecturer for whom I was standing in as Correspondence Courses lecturer didn't recover his health. That left me in charge until 1969, meshing in amazingly well with the work I was doing for eight hours each week as a tutor in English I.

At about this time, the College prevailed upon the three Government Departments to write and organise their own Training Courses, on the grounds that they **must** know much more clearly than we could know what they wanted their officers to do. They could arrange face-to-face instruction in different centres around the state, much more appropriately placed and funded than could S.T.C. In addition, each course would be run with particular relevance to the Department concerned, and they could decide for themselves much more honestly and realistically what was to be the relationship, if any, between training and promotion.

Come to think of it, not altogether unlike the Teaching Service, wouldn't some of you say?

o-o-o-o-o-o-o-o-o-o-o-o-o

The next step towards my move into the English Department of Sydney Teachers' College was taken at some time during 1968, if my memory serves me correctly. I was asked if I'd like to lecture on the poetry of T. S. Eliot, as part of the English Dept. contribution to the Sixth Form Study Day. (Nowadays called Year 12 Study Day?!) It was held in lecture rooms in the University, and the idea was to lecture on books that had been set for that year's H.S.C.

Naturally I felt flattered by being asked to be in it. I accepted the task, and as ever thoroughly enjoyed myself. A day or two later, a senior member of the English staff came to me and said:

"What are you doing in the Education Department of the College, when your Cambridge Degree was in English? And judging purely by your Eliot Lecture on the Sixth Form Study Day, you definitely ought to be teaching in our department!"

And so it happened that at the beginning of 1969 I was transferred to the English Department, to which I belonged until my retirement almost sixteen years later. I was even made permanent instead of temporary!

10. Wesley College

Good heavens! **Now** I discover that I don't want to start on **that** part of the odyssey until I've told you some other things. Really! Signs of a disordered mind? Or just of insistent recollections of a different bunch of students? Whatever the reason, I find myself assailed by powerful remembrances of the students who came to live in Wesley College while they did their Degree courses in the University of Sydney. Maybe they all knew just how memorable they were! Whether they did or not, I'm going to take time out of the S.T.C. saga to tell you of just one or two episodes, events, interviews, conversations etc. that seem to have marked my memory indelibly during the twelve years we had with them.

It was our custom to ask our students to come into residence the weekend before Orientation Week started. That gave us time to make ourselves known to them as a community, likewise for them to get to know one another. Not to mention the lay-out of the College: bathrooms, library, common-room, seminar rooms, and, of course, above all, the kitchen and dining-room! Also to begin to feel at home in their own study-bedrooms before they'd to be used for really serious work after term started in earnest. Wesley specialised in those days in taking in many country students, so this period of 'getting-to-know-you' was of particular importance, and was always extremely fruitful as a settling instrument.

One of the most useful and memorable happenings of those weekends was the session in which the Freshers stood up individually and told us where they came from, which Faculty they were entering, and any other information they wanted to give as to family, school or community experiences.

The first remembrance that leaps to mind comes from such an occasion. I ought to tell you first that we held to an old tradition of wearing undergraduate (or graduate!) gowns to the Evening Meal in the Dining Room. Until these garments had been washed several times, (and as they were made of a cheap, student-affordable black fabric, who'd bother?) they had a highly noticeable, musty, objectionable smell, remarked by all and sundry.

We had in one year a Music student, who told us in her self-introduction that she came from a fairly large family. This had proved to be of great use to her in a quite unexpected way—one she'd be delighted to share with the rest of the student body. As a result of considerable experience in the field of nappy-washing, it had occurred to her (no doubt because of that penetrating smell!) to try soaking her under-graduate gown in a bucket of nappy-treatment solution. The method had been so successful that she'd no hesitation in heartily recommending it. As you can see, I haven't forgotten her tip after over twenty years, even though my silk-corded Cambridge M.A. gown has never needed such drastic treatment—indeed, I've never even had it dry-cleaned since buying it from Ryder and Amies over forty years ago! Tut-tut!

Among the many happy things that the Wesley students did in the course of each year, the College Concert sometimes took pride of place. Naturally its success depended not only on how much talent there was in any particular year, but on how much of that talent could be sought out and persuaded to join in, allowing for the pressures of study. If the pressure of friends was the greater, then it prevailed!

There were students who were musically gifted, who'd been well-taught, who'd played in groups during their school years. Even some who'd only just found out that they could play or sing well since coming to college. Lots of the others were pleased to try their hands at revue-type skills and sketches poking fun at The Establishment in hilarious parodies of lectures, political speeches, School Speech Nights and job interviews. Not The Goodies or Monty Python, of course, but nevertheless highly enjoyable student nonsense. Perhaps more like the Goon Show!

Just one tiny episode refuses to let me complete this Wesley College Students section without giving it a nook or cranny (crook or nanny?) of its own. Very well, you disrespectful niggler, here's what you seem to be asking for. (Never end a sentence with a preposition, June. People will think you don't know your job.)

In the middle of one sketch, and more than once in the general flow of things, one guy kept popping onto the stage in what you could only call 'a disruptive manner'. Every time of course to laughter and applause from the audience. Wasn't that the object of the exercise? What we'd all come for? Finally, to end the show, he emerged in his swimming shorts, a familiar road-sign fastened round his waist warning us that the area was SLIPPERY WHEN WET. The audience held its collective breath for a split second before bursting into gleeful shouts.

There now, impishly persistent impropriety remembered. Satisfied? Comparable recollections ought to have a book of their own, oughtn't they? We can't go on like this all day, or I'll never have room for all those serious professional experiences in the fields of English for Slower Learners, Adult Literacy and Education in T.A.F.E., shall I? Not to mention the **un**serious ones!

11. S.T.C. English Department 1969 to 1985—Adviser

One of the first duties given to me when I became a member of the English Dept. staff in 1969 was that of being Adviser and English lecturer to a Dip. Teach. Primary Group, Section 108. I've been looking up their names in my Record Book; trying to recollect their faces; noting the marks they scored for me in their English assignments; wondering where they all are, and what they're doing these days. Are they still teaching? How many children have they had in the twenty-four years since, and are any of them grandparents?

That group had a special importance for me for all sorts of reasons, not least that through them I had to become familiar with the Primary Curriculum in English; the changes that were being made, or at least tried out, by the forward-thinking souls in the public schools of N.S.W. As my own training and practice up until then had been for and with Secondary and Tertiary students, it was an exciting adventure to find out from the planners, committees, and above all the practising teachers, what progress was being made. I'd **heard of** and **read about** such things as Behaviour Modification, Playways, The Integrated Day, English Through Drama, the Montessori method, Steiner schools, and Small Group work. **But**, until I went with my students in 108 to Demonstration Lessons, and supervised them and others on School Practice twice or three times during that year, all those topics were theory rather than practice to me. No surprise to anybody?!

As their Adviser I learnt a lot about the difficult financial circumstances that beset some of them. How they couldn't find suitable or affordable lodgings in term-time (needed because their homes were too far distant for them to get to lectures in time); the trouble they had sometimes in doing the research necessary for an assignment; above all, the paramount need for evening and week-end jobs, to support themselves.

At times I was reminded of my London girls, and their assertion that 'Life isn't the same for everybody.' Certainly it had never been in any way as hard for me to do my Teacher Training as it was for some of the students who came to me for help and advice in the years between 1969 and 1984.

There are lots of interviews and conversations that spring back into my mind. Here's one of the unforgettable ones.

Judy came to me with what she called "total despair" about her college work.

"I sit there for hours, just staring at the page. Nothing happens in my mind. No thoughts come at all. It's been going on for weeks. What on earth am I going to do?"

"Have you seen your doctor, Judy? Is the problem your health? Could you be anaemic, for instance?"

"I've been under medical supervision for ages. They sent me for psycho-therapy, and some weeks that helps a lot. But not with my college work. Especially not as exams get nearer. I'm sure I'm going to fail."

"Never! You're one of my most gifted students. Why should you fail?"

"Because I've so much on my mind—and because I've never succeeded at anything important so far in my whole life."

"You got your H.S.C. all right, or you wouldn't be here!"

"Yes, I know, but there was a guy who loved me in those days, and that gave me confidence. Since then he's chucked me—says I'll never know how to love **anybody**, I'm so selfish. I don't get it! I did all the housework in the flat, all the shopping, cooking, washing and ironing. All **he** had to do was just to **be** there, like all the others I've tried to live with."

"How many others? Since when?"

"Oh, I've lost count. You see I left home when I was fifteen, and I've lived with different people for the last four years. I can go home any time I want—sometimes I do, and stay for awhile, but not for good."

"What does your mother think of it all?"

"She's wonderful. She understands my problems right through—she's always had enough of her own, so she knows what it's like. Mind you, I've always tried not to upset her with every little thing that bothers me."

"Your father?"

"He shot through years ago. He was an alcoholic. I can understand it now, but when I was fourteen I hated him for it—especially the effect it had on Mum. She kept the house so clean and all. I thought he ought to appreciate her, not knock her about. In the end that's why I left."

"You seem to take after her, don't you? Keeping your place clean and tidy, I mean, and mothering your boyfriends! You must be trying to make yourself indispensable, in the hope they won't leave."

"Funny you should say that! Just what my therapist says. There's one thing—I can't go back to **him** and admit I've failed again, can I?"

"Why not? Isn't that what he's there for?"

"Yes, that's true. He said I was to come whenever I needed to talk to him, or when I felt myself to be slipping down, going on the drugs again—but I can't face him because I know what he'll say."

"Such as?"

"I **am** disappointed in you, Judy. I really thought you had it licked this time!"

"Has he ever said that, or anything like it?"

"No—I'm just afraid this time he might."

"Isn't that more like what you say to yourself? When you get low and think nobody cares for you?"

"Look, I've been so low not even God could love me. I know **He'll** never forgive me, and neither would my Dad if he knew about the drugs. It's been six years now, and I don't believe any more that I'll ever be able to stop. Who'd care if I did, anyhow?"

"Obviously **you** would, or it wouldn't bother you like this, would it? And I would, because I recognise good teacher-material when I see it. Wouldn't you feel life was worth living if you could get more creative writing out of your kids, like the poems you got from them on School Prac. last June?"

"Now there's another funny thing! When I'm out prac. teaching I feel as if I'm in the right place—more sort of worth-while. I reckon I must be still a Primary kid at heart, after all! What a laugh, after all I've been through!"

"Well! **I** know you have a lot of imagination, and you're obviously sensitive and vulnerable. **That's** what puts you on their level. Kids aren't stupid. They can tell who's 'on side', you know! That's why they wrote so well for you."

"It wasn't any effort to sit up late getting lessons ready for them. I didn't need the drugs that month."

"Doesn't that prove you **will** get better in time? If you can get kids to like you and work for you, what's all this 'I'm inferior' stuff?"

"Well, I **am**, aren't I? Or I'd be able to grow up, and stop grabbing after what I can't have. And I'd stop failing in my college work, wouldn't I?"

"You're not going to fail. Go back and talk all this to your therapist, and we'll see what he says. **I'll** bet you get a distinction in your exams. I know you're capable of it in English."

57

"You're just saying that to kid me to keep on. I think I ought to resign from the Course **now,** before I'm further disgraced by being asked to leave."

That interview took a whole afternoon. It left me feeling angry and sad and sorry for the plight of some young folks. Was it circumstance alone that brought someone like Judy down so far? Was she just not tough enough to cope with the world, in spite of her already considerable experience of it? Would she pull through her bitterly low opinion of herself, finding some self-confidence, someone who would really love her and be heartened by her abilities, qualities and tenderness? If all that happened, her potential was enormous. Any teacher who's been through it in Adolescence has a chance of touching kids more deeply, of reaching greater communication with them so that their personal and educational needs can be met and satisfied.

What I had so powerfully hoped for and dreamed of that day had its fruition over a year later. Here's how **that** conversation went.
I caught sight of her at the bottom of the steps leading up to the College library, and instantly noticed the impish smile and lively twinkle radiating from her eyes. What a difference!

"Hi Judy! You look cheerful for a change! What's happened? Got an 'A' on your assignment?"

"Yes, since you ask. Actually on **two** of them! But that's not all the good news—I was just on my way to your office to let you know I'm **better**—I don't have to go back to my therapist any more! Isn't that fabulous?"

"Oh, Judy! That's marvellous news! Do you really feel now that the long haul's over?"

"I'm hoping with all my heart it is, yes. It's been so long since I felt anything like as good as I do now. I can work properly too! Do you remember what I was like twelve months ago when I came to see you about it?"

"Shall I ever forget?! Well, if you're really and truly better, that's one fewer of my charges I need to worry about, eh? I'm so pleased! Best of luck for the exams, anyway."

"Oh, there's one more thing I wanted to tell you. I'm getting married after Christmas. I finally found somebody who's stayed around long enough to get to know me as a person—not just a cook-housekeeper or cot-companion. I'm bound to say that even the drugs didn't reconcile me to being used as a door-mat, although I certainly tried for long enough—over four years, as I seem to remember telling you last August."

"You sure did! Tell me more about 'him', can you? How old is he, and what does he do for a living, if any?"

"He's thirty—and he's a sort of plumber/handyman. Lots of people round our way know him, because he's done their odd jobs pretty well over the last few years."

"How well d'you know each other?"

"He's lived next door for two years, so I'm pretty sure he has no illusions about **me**! And although I wouldn't want to bet on it, I feel that after all the guys I've known and lived with, I've found a good one this time. I only need to look at how my college work's improved. I'm reminded of my H.S.C. year, and how well I went then when I was in a happy relationship. This one's even **more** hopeful, 'cos Bob's so much more mature and supportive. He's actually **proud** of me, and gets as excited as I do when I get good results!"

"That's really great news! There's one thing about him—he should be old enough to know his own mind by now, as far as wives are concerned! And after all you've been through I'd feel pretty sure **you** know what you need in a mate."

"I'd say so!"

"Every happiness for the future, then. See you after the holidays."

I stood there for a moment, thinking, as Judy bounded off up the Library stairs, undeniably full of joyous life and vitality. A far cry from the weeping girl who'd come to see me a year earlier! Her student record at the end of year reads:

Distinction in Class-room Teaching; Distinction in English; Satisfactory in all other Primary Courses.

o-o-o-o-o-o-o-o-o-o-o-o-o

Looking once again this morning through my Mark Book for those years, I find I'd forgotten just how many students from overseas-born families came to us to be trained as teachers. Apart from the fact that I saw no West Indians, and the only Africans I taught came from Egypt, I can't help thinking again what a useful preparation for working in Australia my experience in London was!

An educational problem common to both places arose from that inevitable culture-change experienced by both parents and children of migrant families. The parents, nearly always forced to be or to become working-class, not least because of language barriers, want desperately, believe in, fight hard to get for their children the kind of education that will provide security and upward mobility in the social scale. They are at the same time anxious not to lose the birth-right culture of their homeland, while being fully aware that in the society to which they have come, education has been up to now the key to a secure financial future.

I found out from my migrant-background students, just as I did at Shelburne, that the clash between parents, grandparents and children gets worse as schooling continues. It was bad enough in Primary school, they told me, as nearly all the parents who ever went to school did so under strongly-authoritarian systems. They are sure, therefore, that daily rote-learning and harsh discipline are indispensable features of the learning process. The Australian system, especially in its Primary stages, is far less rigid, and often the migrant parent is deeply worried by a state of affairs that seems so 'permissive' it must surely undermine their children's moral fibre!

As the children reach adolescence, however, they face a rather different, more pressing problem. If they go on with more 'academic' conditioning they **may** qualify for more-highly-paid jobs, but it will be at the expense of emotional closeness to their families. Often they can't bear to lose this warmth and support, especially if they haven't yet managed to make any close Australian friends.

As with my girls in London, their social lives are often more closely controlled than those of their class-mates, following religious, family or ethnic customs. An example might be the degree of supervision or chaperonage of girls, even at student-teacher age. This makes it very hard for them to join in out-of-school trips, visits or camps, including those that are a requisite for the course of study they're pursuing. Such children are in a double bind: wanting to fulfil their parents' ambitions for them, thus partly repaying the huge emotional cost of wrenching up the family's roots to make a better life for them, and at the same time wanting to feel at home in the new community, since this also was the object of the migration exercise. The more at home the children feel, the more they fear the reproaches of their elders.

Too often in those years they cut the knot by leaving school or university before they've completed their courses. They take a job similar to the one their parents do, settling for family unity. Generally the worst they have to put up with after that is the charge of having wasted a precious opportunity for advancement.

Here are a couple of examples of students from migrant families who had quite different personal problems to face in their years of Tertiary study.

Paul's father was dead. He had left to his wife the task of rearing two adolescent boys, both highly intelligent. Being of central European stock, and having had little schooling, and no academic qualifications, she'd worked long hours at sewing to achieve her aim. That was to earn enough money to keep her sons at school until they were eighteen, and then at Sydney University until they had gained their degrees.

The effect on Paul's nature and character was to make him hard and grasping, even though he was grateful to his mother for all her slaving on his behalf, often referring to it in his conversations with me. He had, he said, put all his time, effort and strength into study, doing every night three hours' homework, and twelve hours' worth of it on the weekend. As anyone could see, this schedule left no time at all for social or sporting pursuits. Certainly not for doing anything that would have brought him close to people who **might** have turned into much-needed friends, whether in school or in the wider community. He could never afford to go out anywhere that cost money, anyway.

The net effect of his preoccupation with 'doing well' had been to render him incapable of making friends, or even of relaxing. Just **because** he was so bright intellectually, he was well aware of this fact, and of what a drawback it was to his achieving a happy life. **Not** merely a well-paid one.

In his first year of Uni. he made desperate efforts to get to know people, playing sport, joining clubs, dating girls. But, as he sadly confessed when he came to me for help and advice, no one could stay in his company or cope with him for very long. There was a kind of materialistic arrogance about him that made him inaccessible to friendship, much less to love. The more often he failed to communicate as a human being, showing his needs and having them met, the more bitter and difficult did his personality and path through life become.

Irena's problems arose from a different component of the migrant way of life. She had retained the religious beliefs and practices of her people, and found herself longing for the old traditional ways of life that were based on that moral code. Here's a talk we had in 1970.

"How did you go on your last School Practice? I remember your telling me how nervous you were before starting."

"It was terrific. I really enjoyed it after all, even though I **was** so terrified to begin with! I hadn't expected to be able to teach Science in a co-educational high school, you see."

"Was their own Science teacher a man?"

"Yes, but he was incredibly helpful, considering I must have looked like a helpless female to him!—That's what my brothers said, anyway!"

"Well, Irena, you never act like one that I've ever seen, even though you **are** so pretty!"

"**Do** you mind? Spare my blushes! I must say I was more worried by some of the other members of Staff than I was by any of the kids."

"Why? Didn't they accept you?"

"Oh yes, that side of things was fine. It was the tired, worried, dried-up look of so many of the women teachers that hit me the hardest."

"Thinking that's what **you'll** be looking like in ten years' time?"

"Sooner, I'm afraid. It's so desperately important to me to do well. To become a really good teacher. I expect it's my migrant background; I want to do it for my parents, to justify their faith in me. I guess I'm hag-ridden a bit too much, thinking what a lot it's cost them to educate a **girl**!"

"I can understand **that** all right! **My** father's friends kept on asking him why he was wasting his money on his daughters' schooling when we'd 'only get married and have kids and waste it all'! I have the feeling though that you're wanting a different kind of satisfaction as well. Am I right in thinking you'll want your pupils to look back later in their lives and say: "I owe it all to her!"?"

"Mrs. Webb! How did you guess?—But after that School Prac. I'm beginning to fear what that ambition will cost me. Looking at those women teachers, I'd have to say 'Much too much'. I can see myself making the perfect dried-up school-teacher, getting all my satisfaction in life out of grateful pupils. Having **no** life outside school."

"No boyfriends?"

"No. They do ask me out, but I daren't go. I'm a Christian, you see, and our Church doesn't allow sex before marriage. Neither would my family—they'd disown me. Anyway I don't believe in it myself."

"Irena, you don't have to sleep with a boy just because you go out with him! How will you ever get to know anyone as a friend or companion if you never give yourself the chance to talk to even **one** of them about the important things in life?"

"That's exactly why I worry about it so much. Everybody I know in my Church thinks as I do, but outside that community, the Australians of my age seem to sleep around, and make fun of me because I don't. How I **wish** marriages were still arranged, as they used to be in my grandmother's day. My parents would be sure to find for me a man who'd be a suitable husband. I wouldn't have to go out with him by myself first, and feel so afraid."

o-o-o-o-o-o-o-o-o-o-o-o-o-o

It strikes me as I read through these still-vivid recollections of my Diploma in Teaching students that I failed to mention that I was also given Graduate Diploma of Education classes. Some of the latter had in them students who'd been in my English I tutor-groups between 1966 and '69. It was great fun to renew acquaintance with them, finding out how they'd gone in their Finals, and asking them what had made them decide to become teachers. (Apart from those who were on Teachers' Scholarships, and were therefore bonded to teach, or pay off the bond.)

I was specially interested in the motivation of the non-Scholarship graduates, in view of the amazingly low opinion of Sydney Teachers' College that was fashionable at that period in the ranks of Sydney University graduates! There were even one or two occasions on which I was asked what **I** was doing there, 'in view of the fact,' as they said, 'that you obviously know what **real** life is about.' Doesn't any teacher with a few years' experience?

Oddly enough, it always seemed to me that our Dip. Teach. students had a certain advantage over our Grad. Dip. Ed. students. Namely, that they were with us for three years, during which time they could do six periods of School Practice, gaining confidence, insight into children and classroom expertise. This applied whether they were in Primary or Secondary courses. The Dip. Ed. students had only **one** year with us, giving them only two periods of School Practice. Quite a few didn't find out until their first Prac., at the end of the first term at S.T.C., that three years or more of University work, plus one term of Educational Theory and Practice lectures, had **not** prepared them for the realisation that they didn't like kids in a classroom situation at all. So what on earth were they going to do to earn a living? Were there any other jobs they could hope to get?

One or two of them in the early '70's decided to drop out of their courses anyway, and take off. Here's the farewell conversation I had with the first one to leave at mid-year.

"I just came to say 'Thanks, and see you later'"

"So you've decided to leave us?"

"Yeah. Suddenly hit me this just isn't **me**. You know what I mean."

"What are you planning to do? If you know yet, that is!"

"Just get out of the city for a while—find a job on the land until I've saved up enough to buy five acres or so . . ."

"Sounds good. What made you decide against teaching?"

"That day we were studying a play with you, and you said 'Haven't any of you ever asked yourselves "What am I **doing** here? How did I land up here anyhow?" Remember? You were telling us that writers of the Theatre of the Absurd often pose that question."

"I certainly remember noticing you nodding your head like mad when I asked the question! Made me think 'Oh good! There's **one** who's understood the beginnings of Absurd Theatre at least!"

"Well, that was the moment I got the message. It dawned on me blindingly that it was **only** because I'd won a Teacher's Scholarship that I'd come to the College at all. I hadn't really thought about Teaching as a career. It's just got harder since then to be stuck indoors in lectures, library and labs. Now I realise I've got to get out before I go round the bend. I noticed on Prac. how irritated and fed up some of the teachers were—they didn't seem to **like** their classes at all. Why do people teach if they don't like kids?"

"Who can tell? Perhaps they were pushed into it by their families. By the way, are your parents in agreement with your decision to quit?"

"Not really. Dad's disappointed. He came from the bush himself, and he reckons he wanted something better for me. But **I** reckon there **is** nothing better for me. P'raps I ought to tell him it's in the blood, eh? Inherited from him! We shall see, anyhow. I dare say I'll be back if it doesn't work out. Thanks for all your help this year, especially being willing to listen to us when we've had problems."

There were others who came in on Mature Age scholarships or grants, and for them it was even harder to adjust to Teachers' College routines! Everything depended on what they'd done before in their lives: jobs, marriage, schooling, university work and so forth. For some of them, like Stuart at twenty-one, it was the right move at the right time. In his case it led to a highly-fulfilling career as a Physical Education teacher.

Part of the work in Communication with all classes was to enable them to express themselves effectively in speaking to their pupils, as well as in writing lesson-plans and notes. (Not to mention writing assignments for their lecturers!) I learnt a great deal about Art, Music, Science, Manual Arts and lots of other subjects as my students held forth as requested. Before getting them to 'give a lesson' in their Method subject, I asked them to tell me what they remembered most, or most vividly, from their school days. Nobody ever seemed to dry up when asked for that 'talk'—interesting, that, don't you think?

—Considering how these recollections of mine keep rushing back and swamping my resolutions to be more orderly and proper in setting them down! Not to mention remembering to make the lunch at the right time, do the washing, or clean the house. Dear me, June, priorities **still** no different from how they used to be? You still insist on thinking that People are more important than Things, don't you?—

Back to what Stuart said at one of these 'Introduce yourself and your school-memories' sessions.

"Oh, I couldn't get out of school quick enough. I enjoyed Sport all right,—I was pretty good at it—but one afternoon a week isn't much to push you into trying hard with the rest of the subjects that don't interest you, is it? I just went off up the coast, working my way at odd jobs right round Australia. Didn't let my parents know where I was or what I was doing until I felt ready to settle to something more permanent. In the end I could see I'd have to get **some** qualification or other, so when a mate of mine told me about this P.E. scholarship, I applied for it.

Were my folks ever pleased! Tell you what, though, I feel caged in, here. Less than life-size, somehow. It's funny—I feel a different bloke when I'm on the road. I can hardly wait for the summer break to get off on the bike and up the coast again."

Susan, also 21, recollected her school-days like this:

"I'm sure I spent more time outside the classroom than I did inside. I was always in trouble for mucking up, because I'd finished my work before the others had, and I'd nothing left to do. I used to take in books to read under the desk, but that didn't suit the teachers either, although it did mean I was quiet, not disturbing the rest of the girls, if they'd only let me read. (Shades of Shelburne!) I can still hear one of my teachers saying 'Susan! It's really good you've done your work so fast! Wouldn't it be nice if you were to go over and help one of the slower girls! Such a praiseworthy piece of social service!' It's a wonder to me I ever considered Teaching as a career! Passing the exams to get in here was **easy** compared with trying to visualise myself in front of a class. There's one thing—I doubt whether any of my kids could possibly manage to be as troublesome as I was!"

Kay, 3l, came into our Dip. Ed. year after working in the Public Service since her graduation from University. She spoke as follows in one Speakers' Workshop:

"I didn't mind a bit coming to lectures and doing essays in my Uni. days. That's over ten years ago now, though, and my attitudes have changed, I find. Why don't the lecturers here just give us the list of books and references needed for each topic, and let us get on with the work ourselves? It's such a waste of time and energy to have to sit in a stuffy lecture-room, to listen to somebody talking about a text you could read for yourself in half the time and twice the comfort. If they don't trust us to do the reading and get the assignments in, how can they trust or expect us to be well-prepared, conscientious teachers next year when we go out?"

Before I go on to tell you about the years in which the College set up its Method course in Teaching the Adolescent Slow Learner, offering options in it to all Primary and Secondary Dip. Teach. Courses too, I want to pass on to you a couple of student-success stories.

Not every student who came to talk to me about his/her problems regretted having taken the step of joining the institution. Of these two successful ones, the first made his way in spite of the doubts emanating from his parents.

"It's very good indeed of you to see me. I really don't want to waste your valuable time."

"You're very welcome. It isn't every day I'm given the chance to rave on about Teaching to somebody who genuinely wants to know.—I take it you **do** want to know? Because if not, go now! I warn you I'm an absolute menace to anyone who's undecided!"

"Well, I **am** undecided—that's the whole point at issue—that's why I made an appointment to talk to you. What do you mean when you call yourself 'a menace'?"

"Every year for the past five, I've had somebody come to complain that because I'm enthusiastic about my job, I get them all keen when they'd had no intention of being any such thing. **Then** they feel betrayed and let down when they go out on their next Prac. and find classes not that easy to handle at all."

"It's such an enormous step for me to take, even though I'm under **no** illusion that it's going to be easy at all. You see, I know very well that I'm shy, and find it difficult to get on with people."

"Then for goodness' sake don't go into teaching! What made you think of it in the first place?"

"Largely my doctor. Over the last year or two at Uni. I've had to go to him so often with depression and nervous exhaustion, he's begun to ask me if the course I'm studying is right for me."

"What Degree Course **are** you studying at the moment?"

"Arts/Law. It seemed all right when I started, and my parents were so happy when I made high enough marks in my H.S.C. to get into the Arts/Law faculty quota. They bragged to all their business friends about their clever son."

"So why is it going wrong now, if it is?"

"I feel so isolated. I haven't made any friends in the University, and I hadn't any school-friends to fall back on. I'm an only child, and I've never been able to form relationships easily."

"Worse and worse! How **can** you hope to teach, if you can't relate to people?"

"I don't know—it's a shot in the dark, really, I guess—but I'm pretty desperate to find a way of life that might **force** me to communicate **some**thing to **some**body. As well, I feel as if I mightn't be as short of confidence with children as I am with people my own age."

"All right then, here goes. I'll tell you all I can, and if after that a career in Teaching still seems right for you, go ahead. As far as I'm concerned, of course, there **is** only one worthwhile job in the world, but you could say I'm somewhat biased!"

Eight months later.

"Could I just tell you how delighted I am that you talked to me about the nature of Teaching last year? I couldn't be more pleased that I **did** decide to train as a teacher, and got accepted here as well."

"Is it working out? In spite of all the difficulties?"

"Well, you made **those** so clear, I wasn't under any illusions! Yes, everything's going fine."

"School practice?"

"Even that! I expected the boys to laugh at me, but they don't. Perhaps being older than their usual prac. teacher helps, or maybe I'm in a particularly well-run school. The Staff there are endlessly helpful, and my tutors and supervisors from here give me all the support I need."

"What did your parents say?"

"I think they were taken aback after I'd spent so many years doing Arts/Law, but far from being disappointed, as I'd feared, they were so pleased that I'd found a vocation I could be happy in. They say they can tell the difference in me from a mile away!"

"What does your doctor think?"

"He seems to be satisfied. At least as far as I could tell on the one occasion I've seen him this year. I went back to say thankyou to him for suggesting a change of Course, and a new life. He said I must be a late developer!"

0-0-0-0-0-0-0-0-0-0-0-0-0

The second 'success story' started on a very different note, as you'll see from the tone of her first remark!

"I've a bone to pick with **you**!"

"What have I done now?"

"I came along to this class because I couldn't afford to pay back my bond, and I wanted to stay in Sydney so that I could get on with my M.A. this year. So what do **you** do but get us all enthused about teaching English!"

"Good! What's wrong with that?"

"New ideas, new methods, new ways of getting kids interested in writing, in being creative—I began to think things **must** have changed since I was at school!"

"So?"

"So then I go out on mid-year School Practice, and what do I find? The same dragons in charge, the same dreary buildings, the same boring set books and grammar exercises for junior classes. I'll never forgive you!"

"What was it you mentioned to me, that happened in your last week of prac.? When I came in to observe that final lesson—you said there was something you wanted to know, and would ask me later."

"Oh yes—I **was** going to ask for your help on the matter of what is 'allowed' to a student teacher in a school. Are there any 'understood rules'? What **do** you say when kids ask for your address, cry all over you and insist on giving you a farewell present? Ought I to have stalked out in a dignified manner, as I'm sure any of **my** old teachers would've done? Naturally **I** didn't—I was pretty touched, really."

"I see you were a hopeless failure, just as you said!"

"There was nothing wrong with the **kids**! I never said anything bad about **them**. They were great! Mind you, I got a school in a working-class area like the one I was brought up in, so I'd no problems with reaching the kids. Besides, I remembered all the tricks in the book before they did them."

"Do I gather you were highly popular with your teachers when you were at school?"

"Never out of trouble. Mostly because I was interested only in boys, pop-music and films. Added to which, I used to say what I thought in lessons. Bad luck if it turned out to be different from what the teacher thought, or **wanted** us to say!"

"They must've loved you. Did you get your work done too?"

"When I felt like it. They couldn't fault me there—except for calling me 'pert and precocious', which I certainly was!"

"Did you meet many like you in your classes this prac.?"

"I don't think so, but how could I be sure? **I** used to know perfectly well how to keep out of trouble if I wanted, and I dare say ones like me still do. I should hope so, or what **is** the world of school coming to?!"

"What did you enjoy most about the prac. as a whole?"

"Gradually winning over the naughty ones, and getting really super work out of classes that had started out right against me. Gee, that **was** satisfying." (Shades of Shelburne again!)

"Terrific! Now—what was that bone you came to pick with me?"

There's nothing like letting people bend your ear until they've found their own answers, is there?

12. S.T.C. College Camp—A Very Special Setting for Learning

My first acquaintance with "The College Camp" was in 1969 or 1970, when it was the turn of 'my' Section of Primary students to go there. "Yarrawood" is on the road between Richmond and Springwood, not far from the Yarramundi Reach of the Hawkesbury river. That setting seemed very like a perfect paradise to one who lived and worked inside the University campus at Newtown, though even there too, there was an amazingly beautiful and unexpected setting of trees, grass, flowers, birds and court-yards. Maybe it was the river, maybe the fresher air, maybe the whip-birds that made Yarrawood such a balm to the spirit.

Oh dear! That isn't what I set off to tell you at all! As usual, getting carried away by remembered beauties, feeding again on the experiences that fed me in earlier days. Will you kindly get back to the point, June? **But**, reproving voice, I **have** to tell people who might never have heard of it, how the College Camp came into being a very long time ago, to serve as a base from which students could go out into the tiny local schools to do their periods of practice.

In the years when I first went there as Camp Mum, we were still hiring buses to take the students out from the city to Yarrawood, then on a daily basis to ferry them out to those same schools. Who knew which schools would be in need of a teacher by the time the present trainees graduated? How many of them had ever seen in operation a one-teacher or two-teacher school, where children from five to twelve years of age had to be occupied, taught, encouraged and prepared for High School, all at once?

I, for one, never had seen such a sight—one that inspired me to wish I could start all over again! Even after all these years, amidst fears that those fantastic small country schools could never continue to be funded ('cos they're not **economic**, you see!) I warm to the memory of Wilberforce, Ebenezer, Sackville, Colo, Portland (whether that should be Lower Portland, I've forgotten.)

Apart from its ideal situation for tennis, hockey, football, swimming, athletics, orienteering, and generally scrambling round the landscape, the Camp offered all manner of resources for Painting, Sculpture, Crafts made from materials collected around the place, and lots of Drama possibilities. We played table-tennis together, wrote doggerel about each day's activities, had old students to come in as guest-speakers from the coal-face (chalk-face?) and organised an entertainment for the last night of the Camp.

I fancy that the time I **most** distinguished myself was during such an 'entertainment'!! It was taken for granted that any members of Staff who were in attendance would contribute **something** to the evening's shenanigans—and anyway, we had to show off, if possible, didn't we? At that very first camp, the other lecturer in residence was Denis Condon, a member of the Music Department—a fact of which I was unaware. I'd only realised in the course of the week that he seemed to be good at playing the piano, and as at that time I still had enough of a voice to sing, he and I agreed to perform a couple of English folk-songs as our contribution to the entertainment.

When we'd done our bit, (much to the disapproval of one or two of the girls in my Primary section, who said: "the tone of those words is so crude and cruel! How **can** you sing them as if you **mean** them?") I turned to Denis and said "You **do** play well!" To which well-meant compliment he replied "I should hope so! Not **too** bad, these days, I suppose." It was only after **that** episode that I found out he was a Lecturer in Music, and had always, from being a small boy, been a talented pianist!

I mustn't leave my recollections of those early Primary camps without recording how impressed I was by the kinds of activity the Science lecturers used to organise. One year Toni O'Neill set for each pair of students the task of measuring out one square metre of ground, mostly in the treed areas of the place. In the course of the day, they were to count up, collect where possible, record and draw or photograph their findings. The pairs then made a more permanent display of the insect, plant and animal inhabitants of 'their' patch of ground, with the object of using such a display as a teaching tool on their next school practice.

I can still see and hear their astonishment at the crowded life to be found in such a small space. No more surprised than I was, I assure you! How I wished I'd had a teacher of Botany, Biology or Ecology like Toni!

Come to think of it, the great advantages of 'a week at Yarrawood' showed themselves best after we had started the Special Education courses. **There** we could work on and demonstrate practically lessons in every subject. This might therefore be a good time (at last!) to pass on to my recollections of that time, when all I'd learned about the needs of Slower Learners, Children With Learning Difficulties and Teachers Who'd Never Been Trained To Cope With Such, turned out to be more than useful: more like indispensable.

13. English for Special Education 1971-1981

As a result of their experiences on School Practice, more and more students came to ask their supervisors and Method lecturers what they were supposed to do with the children in their classes who didn't seem able to learn much, if anything, of what the teacher expected the class to learn. The students in Diploma of Teaching, Secondary, or in Graduate Diploma of Education, Secondary, had even greater problems than did the Primary students. They were finding in their High School prac. classes some pupils who were **still** unable to read. At least not the texts that were required for class-work.

Those students had never been trained to teach Reading, whereas that study was an integral part of the Primary course. In one sense, you can see that it didn't make things any easier for the Primary groups. Knowing that they were **supposed** to be able to handle anything at all that might crop up in Primary teaching, whatever the age of the class, they could do one of several things. First, they asked for help from the regular class teacher, on whose kids they were practising.

If no joy from that quarter, they could try as I did at Shelburne to think up niftier ways of presenting their material, hoping to find a way through the thicket. Third, they had to survive a period of self-condemnation for not solving the problem. ("I'm supposed to be the teacher, aren't I? What's the matter with me, and what will my Supervisor say?")

After going through all that, and possibly more, some of them showed a real gift for reaching the Slow Learner. The college was able to set up and fund two whole groups: one in third-year Dip. Teach. Primary (later offered from second-year onwards), and one in Dip. Ed. Secondary, where T.A.S.L. (Teaching the Adolescent Slower Learner) was offered as a Method course, in the same way as were T.E.S.L. and T.E.S.O.L. (i.e. Teaching English as a Second Language, and Teaching English as a Second or Other Language). Not too many of our graduates took both these courses, but lots took T.A.S.L. together with their other Method courses, e.g. English, History, Art, Music, Science, Maths., Drama.

So much of my previous teaching and family experiences now proved to be relevant and useful. As I indicated in an earlier recollection of my shattering start with my 'Scripture' work at Shelburne, my Australian students were not really disposed to believe me when I told them I'd certainly been through some of the self-questioning they were going through.

"Oh, come off it," they retorted. "How did you ever get appointed to this place if you weren't able to maintain discipline? **That** seems to be all we're judged on when we go out on Prac. If you were our Prac. supervisor, wouldn't **you** expect us to have our classes working quietly? All sitting in neat rows?"

Would I? As the Slower Learner courses progressed, and I **did** get the chance to take the students out to Demonstration lessons and then to supervise them on School Practice, most of them realised that I was in the habit of telling them the truth. Also, that any suggestions I might make for solving problems with classes or individuals were not abstracted from Education text-books.

It took some of the Graduate Dip.Ed. students in particular quite a while to accept 'different' ways of dealing with pupils who had learning difficulties. After all they had themselves been pretty bright at school, or they'd never have gone to Uni. anyway, and probably wouldn't have wanted to go. So how could they be expected to tune in to the needs of kids of a very different ilk?

Surprisingly often (or is it, in your life-experience?) they became interested in helping such kids if there was one known to them personally, either in the family or living in the neighbourhood.

Coming back to my Olivetti after a few days away from it, I find I've been thinking of one of my T.A.S.L. students from the class of 1977. He was the first one ever to question the assumption that it's vital to teach Slower Learners to **read** first of all. I came to see his objection as a very proper concern, in view of the methods of instruction that exist nowadays: not only on audio and videotape, radio and television, but also in the excellent films that are available to teachers from the Resource Services Dept. at Burwood.

But, at the time when Bob declared so definitely that we teachers think it essential for **everybody** to read purely because **we** learned all we know from books, passed our exams because we were 'good at book-learning', and now get paid for insisting that Reading is the sine qua non of education—well! I was proper fazed! So much so that I turned to the rest of the group, asking them for more contributions on the subject. I didn't feel at all confident that I hadn't become thoroughly old-fashioned, merely the product of the way **I** had been trained and conditioned.

Naturally, after several years' practice, most of the members of that T.A.S.L. group knew very well how to give to any lecturer answers that would be gratifying and acceptable. Hadn't they always found that the grades they were given depended entirely on their skill in just that direction? So those who spoke at all agreed that **all** pupils needed to be able to read well enough to make sense of **any** subject.

"Even in Maths and Science," they said, "the questions in exams and the info. in text-books are all set in **words** as well as figures, aren't they? For instance, the instructions themselves will run: 'Solve the following problem, equation, reaction,' and so forth."

Not to mention the sheer necessity of making sense out of the instructions on packets, bottles of medicine, forms that have to be filled in. Even those applying for bank-loans and car and home insurance contracts!

It so happens that I was visiting my daughter a couple of years ago, fairly near to where Bob was teaching. I rang him up to see if he was still of the same mind about book-reading, and if so, to ascertain what methods of teaching he'd found useful and preferable in the intervening twelve years, during which he'd worked in Special, Aboriginal and Technical College Education.

"Well," he replied, "in view of the fact that I've written a book on the history of T.A.F.E. in this district, and had it published, you can judge for yourself what I now think about the value of teaching Reading!"

He next reminded me of the time in 1977 when he'd told the class that his nick-name at school had been 'Boof-head'. I had to confess to him that I'd had no idea what that meant, until comments made by members of the class gave me a clue! It now occurs to me that if Bob had had a Classical education, his nick-name might have been 'Bucephalus', don't you think?

o-o-o-o-o-o-o-o-o-o-o-o-o-o

Several of the Inner City schools within easy reach of the College had at least one Slow Learner class. Most had more than one. They proved to be endlessly helpful in the field of Special Education. We went to them to see Demonstration lessons, where our students watched experienced teachers handling the problems and difficulties in learning faced by G.A. (General Activities) classes in English, Maths and Science. Cleveland Street, Newtown, Bourke Street, Enmore High School: these were all schools to which we turned for information, advice, comment, on what we were trying to do to prepare students to go out into the schools as trained Special Ed. teachers.

Apart from accepting students for six or eight weeks of the year to do their School Practice, Enmore offered a specially helpful service. The school had an Annexe in Metropolitan Road, at a distance of a hundred or two metres from the main school in Edgeware Road. Classes used to stream down at intervals from the main building when it was their time for Manual Arts, Personal Development or Migrant English. (Maybe other things as well—'s hard to remember after twelve years!)

The Master in charge of the Annexe at that time, Jack Busby, was not only a remarkable teacher of Disadvantaged, Migrant and Slower Learners, especially in Maths. He offered to our T.A.S.L. students an inestimable opportunity. They were invited to the Enmore Annexe in any conveniently manageable spaces they might have in their timetables, to experience for several weeks together just what

'Teaching the Adolescent Slow Learner' meant in practice. Those who took advantage of Jack's offer became 'Teacher's Aides', finding ways of working individually with kids who only needed more time and attention from a concerned adult in a one-to-one relationship. **Then** they could make progress in Reading, Maths, Science, Social Science and Life Skills.

Not only did it help the kids, and enable the teacher to move ahead more quickly with what he/she wanted to do with the class as a whole, it gave the College students some real, concrete ideas for making teaching aids, games, films, local history projects and excursion objectives. Any of these they could use in their own later periods of School Practice, and also, of course, in any G.A. classes in the schools to which they might be appointed after finishing their College training.

As you can tell, I remember Enmore with special gratitude and affection. Balmain High and Cleveland Street taught us lots too. In fact I can hear, popping up in my memory's A.T.M., a prompter who's saying "You haven't forgotten, have you, how thrilled you were when the Clevo Special Ed. teacher told you that, for the first time ever, boys who'd started as migrants in the G.A. class has passed in Greek, Economics, Maths and Science in the H.S.C.?"

No, I must say I don't seem to have forgotten **much** about those years of teaching English for Special Education, for all that at the same time I was having a highly-fruitful relationship with English / History classes who weren't intending at all to specialise in teaching slower learners. I must tell you later on about a lecture period in which a Primary Dip. Teach. section and I were doing Drama, right next door to a Maths lecture—in an echoing pre-fab at Carillon Avenue, too!

Before I get too far away from the Special Ed. work, though, I must record the opening lecture I gave whenever I was starting a course with a new group. I've even been known to be asked to give it as a guest lecturer to one of my colleagues' classes! Here goes.

0-0-0-0-0-0-0-0-0-0-0-0-0

"Did any of you study George Bernard Shaw's play 'Pygmalion' when you were at school? Most people seem to know 'My Fair Lady', the musical and film that were made from it, but the play itself doesn't seem to be as much studied in high school as it was in my distant youth.

I ask if you know it because I want to begin my lecture with a quotation from Act Five—part of a conversation between Eliza and Colonel Pickering. It has always seemed to me to hold the secret of Educating—most of all of how to deal with kids who are having problems at school, so have been put into 'the Class for Slow Learners'. Thus classified, labelled and pigeon-holed, it would be surprising if their self-esteem survived the treatment. Would yours have done?

As Eliza asks Pickering:

Liza: "Do you know what began my real education?"

Pickering: "What?"

Liza: "Your calling me Miss Doolittle that day when I first came to Wimpole Street. That was the beginning of self-respect for me. And there were a hundred little things you never noticed, because they came naturally to you. Things like standing up and taking off your hat and opening doors . . ."

Pickering: "Oh, that was nothing."

Liza: "Yes: things that showed you thought and felt about me as if I were something better than a scullery-maid; though of course I know you would have been just the same to a scullery-maid if she had been let into the drawing room. **You** never took off your boots in the dining room while I was there."

Pickering: "You mustn't mind that. Higgins takes off his boots all over the place."

Liza: "I know. I am not blaming him. It is his way, isn't it? But it made **such** a difference to me that you didn't do it. You see, really and truly, apart from the things anyone can pick up (the dressing and the proper way of speaking, and so on), the difference between a lady and a flower girl is not how she behaves, but how she's treated. I shall always be a flower girl to Professor Higgins, because he always treats me as a flower girl, and always will; but I know I can be a lady to you, because you always treat me as a lady, and always will."

So if 'the difference' between how people **are** and how they turn out depends **not** on 'how he/she behaves' but on 'how he/she is treated', what does that tell us about students of all ages who have trouble with school instruction? (You'll notice I didn't say "school **learning**". Children never fail to learn the hidden curriculum in school, namely: "What am I supposed to do? How can I please them so's they'll like me? What's **expected** of me in this place? What is it my parents sent me here for?")

What **are** the Teacher-expectations and the Parental-expectations that govern so powerfully the roles a child may play? And where did our society's judgments and standards of what constitutes "School Success" come from? Before we examine those areas, let's have a look at some of the other factors involved in producing 'Slower Learners'.

We'll start with any possible genetic components. If there is in the family impaired hearing, damaged heart, lung or digestive function, poor eyesight, a baby may well inherit one or more of these handicaps. As that puts it in line with the rest of the family, any problem may well not have been noticed in the period before the child starts school. Certainly not enough to account for any difficulties experienced in class or playground. It isn't bad behaviour, naughtiness or wilfulness if a child can't **see** writing or drawing on the chalkboard, (so seems to be 'always talking', asking a neighbour's help), or sits perpetually sideways, uncomfortably, because only **one** ear can hear clearly enough what the teacher is saying. Watch out for these signals of distress from any of the pupils you teach: they are cries for special help.

There are other factors apart from inherited handicaps that can lead to the creation of a slow learner. Perhaps the child wasn't wanted at all, the mother having had already as many children as she can cope with. This is, of course, especially possible in circumstances of great poverty, overcrowding and malnutrition. There are still children who arrive at school, not having had anything to eat since the previous day. One or two schools try to organise a breakfast program for such of their kids as are in this kind of need. That's good, but you can imagine just how much poor nutrition contributes to slowness of development, and therefore to insurmountable hurdles in the path of trying to meet society's expectations of school performance. And we haven't even spoken yet of the kind of oxygen-starvation leading to brain-damage that can ensue from the trauma of a really hard birth.

Just one more note we might make on this area of new-borns and young babies that bears on slow development. If, for whatever reason, a baby is amazingly quiet, sleepy, "good",—in fact 'no trouble at all'— parents may well be delighted at first, especially if all their friends are envious! However, if the baby continues to be not just quiet, but positively lethargic, sitting up, crawling, standing, walking and talking 'much later than other kids', the tendency of the parents may well be not to bother stimulating this 'non-reacting' child of theirs. Why play with, buy toys for, recite nursery-rhymes to, point to objects while saying their names (for all of us our first life-lessons ever!) if you don't get enough response from the baby to encourage you to keep going? Why not just be thankful that you can get on with other jobs you have to do? Such a conclusion would be a real shame—these kids need **more** stimulation, not less; **more** loving attention and faith in their potential than are needed by all those lively, bright youngsters to whom our relatives and visitors are drawn as if to magnets!

Odd, when you come to think of it—the same's true in the classroom, isn't it? Teachers are engaged by and react much more happily to their bright kids. Sometimes they even remember to be thankful for those class-members who are "no trouble at all. Slow, you know, not likely to get very far up the ladder—but absolutely **no** bother."

These are the kids you'll be faced with if you get a Special Ed. class. Or if you're appointed to a school that imagines it doesn't **have** any Slow Learners, you'll find them in the bottom stream.

Incidentally, has anyone among you recently walked past a crowd of youngsters picking up sides ready for a team-game or sport? You may even remember the process from your own school-days. Was there somebody, or maybe more than one, waiting right to the end, hoping to be picked? Did either of the 'captains' say "Well, **we** don't want that dummy on our side. It's somebody else's turn to put up with him/ her. Can't bat, can't bowl, can't run, can't even be sure to take an easy catch. Hopeless!" No peer-group wants an inept team-member. So peer-group expectations come into the question of "What makes a kid a slow learner?"

Often, too, teachers are given such big classes that unless they've had training in Special Education they can't tell the difference between the bored, bright, insolent, rebellious student and the slow learner who's struggling desperately. This state of affairs produces an attitude and reaction on the teacher's part that's very likely to increase the sense of failure and lack of self-worth in a slow learner, who seems to cop it from all sides.

So we see that parent, peer-group and teacher expectations all contribute to produce the 'defeated' Slow Learner, who by definition needs **more time**, and above all **concrete** demonstration, not **abstract** explanation, of whatever it is you want him/her to learn.

So much for the elements that create problems for learning. **How do we turn the expectation of failure into the experience of success**? This is, after all, what this course was designed to tackle, isn't it?

1) Structure all the tasks you set for them in very small steps, so that there's a better chance of ensuring success at each stage. Praise them for everything they tackle rightly and well, however long it takes them, and however slowly they get the hang of the job. Above all, cure yourself of our inbuilt tendency to think of how quickly you, your brother, or **any** sharp kid of your acquaintance could do the

work. Keep remembering that it takes a good teacher to find the key to unusually stiff locks. Bright kids only need the teacher to point them in the right direction—they'll do their own unlocking. The treasure within is from the same store, whether slow or quick to reach.

2) **Change** their learning experiences, so that the Slow Learner **can't** say any longer: "I've tried to do that before, and I failed, as the teacher made very loud and clear. I'd rather not try at all than fail again." How can one change that experience?

If it's at all possible, change the environment in which you work with them, so that no 'failure-expectation' can be reliably set up in their minds. The classroom itself can be transformed by pictures, posters, hangings, models, charts—all these made by the students in their Art and Craft periods. If you teach in Primary, or have a G.A. (General Activities) class of your own, such Art and Craft work will be fitted in with your other subjects, and can very well reflect whatever topic you are dealing with at the time.

I've seen G.A. rooms turned into Space Ships, Under-water Kingdoms, Shops, Arcades, Gardens, Farmyards and Villages from all parts of the world—all constructed out of paper, foil, cardboard, egg-cartons and drink-cans. Depending on the weather, lots of your Drama, Discussion and Film-making work can be done out of doors, too.

3) If in spite of all your efforts to 'change things', you realise that for the kids in your class "School" equals "The place where I always feel stupid", think hard about the possibilities of making **Visits** and Excursions. Obviously, where you could take them will depend on the local surroundings of the school to which you're appointed after college, but here are some ideas, anyway.

a) Places where there is **water,** e.g. beach, river, lake, creek, dam, canal. Your allies in an excursion to one of these places would be staff-members who teach Geology, Marine Biology, Social Studies, P.E. and Art.

What you bring back will lead to **talking**, which you can put on the tape-recorder, **reading** more about what was seen, and **writing** from the stimulus of the visit itself. Also for 'Making a Report' by putting together tapes, photographs, written records and objects brought back. Such a display can be shown to other classes, set up in an open area for the rest of the school to see, and be mentioned in Assembly. All of which can build up the self-confidence and self-esteem of the so-called Slow Learner.

b) Local '**making-places**'—e.g. factory, pottery, bakery, stud, winery, dairy, piggery, cabinet-maker's, stone-mason's, cotton mill. Plus any Tech. classes there may be that are willing to show your class carpentry, joinery, metal-work.

c) Exhibitions of **anything** that are accessible to you, e.g. cars, caravans, boats, agricultural machinery, animal shows, manufacturers' promotions, pictures, arts and crafts, technical design—anything at all that they will **talk** about, take pictures of, **increase their repertoire** of experience of the world and give them an idea of the multifarious jobs people do.

Working out the cost of travel to an exhibition, the distance in kilometres from the school and their homes, the cost to the makers of setting up such an exhibit, plus what they may expect to get out of it all in profit—all these things are practical, relevant **number** work, as well as being abundantly useful material for writing up reports and records. Usually kids can see that this isn't merely classroom 'busy work', designed to keep them occupied and out of the teacher's hair, but real-life stuff that may well be useful to them in later years.

d) **Films and Plays**—however 'suitable' or 'unsuitable' they may be considered to be, they widen the Slower Learner's horizons, can lead to a shift of view-point, shed some light for them, providing experiences for them to discuss and write about. Television can be used in the same way, and nowadays much more cheaply!

So now the big question is "What will you and they get from all this exhausting business?"

1. **Enjoyment** first. Watch that it is so, for this may be the whole difference from 'school' as they've so far known it.

2. **Experience** they might otherwise never get. As a friend of mine found to her astonishment when she took her class from Camperdown to visit Circular Quay. Not one of them had been to see the Harbour before that occasion.

3. **Talk**—a vital part of language development. New vocabulary, new sentence constructions may well be needed to describe the new things they have done and seen, and you may have to supply them. **But** it's when they themselves **need** those words that they're truly open to learning and remembering them.

4. **Art and Craft** work arising from the visits, maybe using materials gathered and brought back. Painting, drawing, illustrating, making models, puppets, collage, 'books'—all can result. If there is no provision in your school for a General Activities class as such, enlist the co-operation of the Art Department staff and work as a team on the upshot of your visit projects.

5. **Dramatization** of situations encountered while on the excursion. (More of this later.) For now, if you went to the sea or another kind of water, you could use appropriate music to which to dance, act, mime, do exercises to re-create the feelings experienced on the trip— probably after discussing them.

6. **Writing**—**after** doing "all of the above", when the question can be asked "How are we going to make a record of what we all saw and did?" Here come into play the photographs, paintings, models, tapes etc. of which we spoke earlier. In time, if their relationship with you, and their increasing interest and enjoyment lead them that way, the more able students will **want** to write up accounts of visits, or poems arising from them.

Nick Otty, in his book "Learner Teacher", reports an almost unstoppable flow from one previously-non-performing student, once his interest and imagination had been aroused. And David Holbrook, in "English For The Rejected", found personal experience and imaginings, hopes and fears the most fruitful sources of writing improvement and self-expression for his class of Slow Learners. I hope it's totally clear to you all that there's no percentage in 'getting kids to sit down and write—it keeps the room quiet'—as has been and maybe still is too much the objective in schools.

What to do about those who aren't that far on in writing yet?

a) Find out what they want to express. Tape it, or write it down.

b) Find or draw strip cartoon pictures, stick men, magazine cut-outs or photographs. Put them on a scroll-chart pinned to the wall-board, all with spaces underneath in which captions can be written—plus at least one extra line-space. Tell you why.

c) Ask them what captions will best fit each illustration. Which do they want? Write those captions up, then get the producers of the ideas to copy your caption on the line you have provided extra on the wall-chart. **Then**, in the next stage of encouragement, suggest that it would be good if **your** writing didn't appear on their work. "I could write the captions on separate pieces of paper for you to copy straight into your books, once you've stuck a picture in, or drawn one, couldn't I?"

d) Next, encourage them to invent **and** write down some captions for themselves, perhaps using words they can see on the class wall-chart you made together. Tell them to ask you for help in writing only **new** words they want to use and don't yet know how to spell.

e) After the 'caption stage', (which may last for weeks or months) comes a 'short sentence' stage, in which some of them will feel more secure if they still have an accompanying picture, whereas others will want to write what they're thinking and feeling directly, without a visual focus. You'll soon find out which is which if you've obtained their trust.

Build up a 'book', stitched or sticky-taped together. This they can **read** because they **wrote** it, and because it's about **their** experience, either first-hand or from story-telling time. Do plenty of that, won't you? For breaks, for fascination, for bringing the class together, to ease tensions when the going is hard. **Do** get good at it. Even at High School level, where we're dealing with Adolescent Slow Learners, reading aloud or telling in serial form a story that is relevant to their lives does great things, so I found.

For any further development of creative writing, get your pupils to use trial-paper for a first go. They all seem to have been conditioned to want to see 'a neat, fair copy' in their 'proper books', not spoilt with a stack of formal correction marks. Don't be afraid to break off, go outside, have some fresh air and a run round, or put on a record and dance in the aisles! You'll be surprised by the renewed vigour with which they'll return to their writing.

As for possible themes on which they might well **want** to write their own books, here are one or two that I've found rewarding and stimulating even at Tertiary level, not only at Primary and Secondary! "School" (Always amazingly productive, if not usually reassuring!) "My Family" "Odd People I've Met" "Where I'd Rather Be Just Now".

DRAMA As I said earlier, there are one or two more things to be noted on this topic, especially the Drama that arises naturally out of excursions. Not to mention its usefulness when you're working up to one. If you discuss and visualise things that might possibly happen on the trip, then act them out, it takes away the sting and fear of unfamiliarity. This can help a lot, as kids, especially those with Learning Problems, are often embarrassed in strange places. Not really knowing how to behave, they giggle, push, mock-fight and talk loudly to give each other a sense of group security—shutting an alien world out of their charmed circle. Facing up to possible situations beforehand in socio-drama helps to defuse them.

Likewise, if embarrassing situations **did** crop up unforeseen, it lays the ghost to re-enact the scene on returning to the classroom.

One colleague of mine pretended not to know her kids on one outing. They were making such a racket on the bus that one angry old lady and the conductor too started asking "Where are these brats from? What are they taught in school nowadays? No manners!" As the kids had already distinguished themselves by running along the Domain Walkway and knocking somebody down, their teacher wasn't feeling too comfortable at having decided to take them out on a visit for the first time.

When they got back to school, they found that impersonating the people they'd met and variously offended gave them much more insight into adults' feelings and expectations than they'd had up to then! Does anyone remember the scene in "To Sir with Love" where some of the passengers on the London Underground make racist and offensive remarks about the West Indian man who seems to be accompanying a number of white teenagers? And one of the girls says "Do you mind? He's our teacher!" There's a terrific growth in imagination if anyone has to act the role of another person, necessitating new vocabulary, new body language, a new way of looking at televised drama and films.

All that as well as the social training and growth in self-esteem so vitally required by all children, and most of all by the ones labelled 'Slower Learner'. Applying for jobs, having interviews, learning how to face using the telephone for unpleasant tasks such as making a complaint, addressing 'superiors' (in any walk of life)—all these can be role-played. Drama is an invaluable resource for developing self-confidence, body-awareness, vitality and self-esteem in the slower-learning child.

In the end, increasing their personal resources may sum up all that we as teachers **can** do, while being especially careful not to give unrealistic expectations for the future to those whom Society is always going to regard and treat as inferior.

Which brings me back to what Eliza Doolittle said in my opening quotation from Shaw's "Pygmalion" . . . "Apart from the things anyone can pick up . . . the difference between a lady and a flower girl . . . (between a bright kid and a slow learner?) is not how she behaves, but how she's treated."

Are we agreed?

o-o-o-o-o-o-o-o-o-o-o-o-o

Remembering and writing about that opening lecture of mine on the College's course in Special Education, and noticing how much Drama work figured in it, I'm reminded that I promised myself and you that I'd tell you about the time I was taking one of my Primary groups for Drama in one of the pre-fab. classrooms at Carillon Avenue. It has always been my style when lecturing in or teaching a practical subject, not to tell my students "This is what to do with your Primary classes." It seemed to be much more useful and instructive for them to know what to do with their kids if they'd actually been through the motions, actions, speech, of improvising the drama themselves.

On this occasion, after the class had sorted itself out into small groups, each discussing what story they wanted to act, it was decided that a storm at sea, creating a shipwreck, from which all survivors would land on an island where hostile inhabitants would make life difficult for them, was the piece they wanted to do. It would be a splendid preparation for their up-coming School Practice period, and everybody settled in with a will to work out how to get the storm-effects and struggling-to-the-island actions that they wanted.

We moved the chairs and tables about, and I squeezed myself into a corner at the back of the room, squatting on the floor with my back against the wall, notebook at the ready so as to be able to write comments and suggestions as the drama was played out.

The play had reached the moment when the hostile inhabitants brandished their weapons, raising truly chilling war-cries. These yells were, if possible, even louder than the racket that had been made by the storm at sea in the earlier section. For second-year students, it was a tremendous enactment. They were wholly absorbed and enthralled by what they were doing.

Then came one of the most memorable happenings of my time as a lecturer. A sudden hush fell over my group, because they could see something which I, from my corner on the floor, could not.

Into the unexpected quiet came the sound of a polite, worried, gentle voice. "Isn't there a lecturer with you? I'm trying to give a Maths lecture next door, and in all this row you're making I can't hear myself speak!"

What a wonderful question to have asked of one's class! Fair made my day, it did! Of course I rose to my feet and apologised, promising that we'd cut down on our sound-effects from then on.

Now why should that episode have made me feel so giggly and pleased with life? I'm sure I ought to have felt ashamed of myself, no? Such uninhibited doings are all very well, but really! Not in echoing places like prefabricated classrooms, eh?

14. The very special time when the Overseas Teachers came to us

In 1991 I travelled to Sydney to attend a reunion that was truly wonderful. Those who organised it and attended were overseas-trained teachers for whom the College had been asked in 1978 to set up 'Conversion Courses'. These courses lasted for two years each, and were designed to enable qualified and practising teachers from other countries to adapt to the Australian style of classroom practice, while they worked for several periods a week on their own English-language skills. Diana, the lecturer who was specially appointed to coach them in this area of Migrant English, became their much-loved helper and champion. Without her expertise and unfailing application, their chances of teaching children in English, in our multi-cultural, multi-racial Primary classrooms would have been much slimmer.

I wasn't offered the chance of taking the first group for English Method lectures, although I got to know many of them as the year wore on. They were so gifted, so open, so experienced, so hard-working, so mature, so determined to succeed. Although the Department had insisted that they be trained for Primary teaching only, some of them had been in their own countries not only High School teachers but also Demonstration Teachers for their local Institute of Education or Teacher Training. As always, I'm sure I learnt as much from them as they did from the College, while recognising that those courses gave them the only chance they had to work here in the System.

You can imagine, therefore, how happy I was to be given the option of lecturing on Primary English Method to the 1979 intake, especially as it turned out to be the last one. No more funds were forthcoming.

The first thing I wanted to know from that whole class was purely for my own information, so that I could structure the Method Course to suit their needs. What were the methods of teaching they had used in their countries of origin?

Constantine from Greece told us he was used to teaching in a far more structured and authoritarian environment than that which he'd observed in Australian classrooms. Each day he would present his pupils with a lesson that was to be recited and learned by heart. They would learn it overnight for homework, and would be required to chant it in unison the following morning in class. He would pick out one or two to repeat the rote-learning individually, so that no-one would be tempted not to get it by heart, hoping to be covered by the sound of the others. (Reminded me of our singing lessons in High School, when we were practising for Speech Day! We **too** were supposed to have memorised our bracket of songs, but I'm sure I wasn't the only one who mouthed some word-shapes, hoping to look convincing!)

Judith, Fabiola and Carmen, from Chile and Argentina, presented a very different image of **their** training and practice. They hadn't had a lot to say during the first week's lectures, being accustomed, as they said, to letting the men have their say before the women ventured to join in! It was, therefore, not until we started on 'Picture Talks' for Infants level that I found out how perfectly easily the South American teachers related to their classes in an informal way. Judith, and later also Barbara Paredes, were so good in that area that I wanted to know how come it was so—having fat-headedly imagined until then that Playways, Learning Through Drama, the Open Classroom, Small Group Work, The Integrated Day were all recent developments in Primary Education. All to be found only in English-speaking backgrounds of course! And I'd thought I wasn't prejudiced!

To be told that Chilean teachers had for years been working in this informal manner wasn't the only surprise that group gave me, either. How come I'd 'forgotten' about Maria Montessori in Italy? Jean Piaget in Switzerland? Paulo Freire in Brazil? Not to mention the work done by Rudolf Steiner.

One of the women who didn't stay with us for long was Elizabeth from Russia. (Oh dear, I'm not sure now—I can see her face and her warm smile, but her country of origin has escaped me—please forgive me, dear lady). Like so many of our 'Overseas students', Elizabeth was teaching her own language at Beginner, Secondary and Tertiary levels on University Extra-Mural courses, and she couldn't face two years' training at S.T.C. to end up qualified only to try to cope with General Primary teaching.

At that time Australia was developing a multicultural education policy, and the authorities were keen to introduce Community Languages into Primary schools. Several of our Migrant Teachers already taught in 'Saturday Schools' where languages of the different cultural groups in our community were offered. That made them ideal candidates for starting the new program in our Public Schools in those neighbourhoods where there was a preponderance of children from the same ethnic background. Not only would those families be happy with such an arrangement: many others in the local community wanted to share in the language and culture of the 'New Australians', and were delighted for **their** children to learn a new language, and to have such an opportunity to communicate with their classmates.

Once or twice each year we had a party in one of the Commonrooms of the College, either at Carillon Avenue or in the University Grounds building. The students brought in food from their varied cultural traditions, and also records of music to dance to, likewise. I mightily enjoyed both food and music, and since at one stage of my (mis-spent?) youth I'd been a keen dancer, I didn't want my overseas friends to think of me only as a staid English lecturer, did I?

Unfortunately for my attempts to come up to scratch, in order to impress them with what I could still do, I hadn't allowed for the fact that the bilateral hip-replacements I'd needed five years earlier seemed to be still affecting the degree of rotation I could achieve! Fabiola, who was organising the South American dance-music, shook her head and addressed me regretfully, with a smile but very firmly.

"**Move** your **hips!**"

Just when I thought I **was** doing, too!

When it came to the part of the course that dealt with Children's Literature, I was talking to them about the range of books, stories, nursery-rhymes and so forth that we use for Story-time and Reading in

Primary work. Again I met a fascinating aspect of cultural difference. Each of the class-members in turn told us a story, or referred to one they'd heard on their last School Prac. In the course of the discussion, I mentioned some of the favourite children's stories in the English tradition that often get used for pantomimes around Christmas time. Cinderella, Jack and the Beanstalk, Mother Goose, Aladdin were some of the examples I quoted.

At this point there was a really serious objection made by Adnan, a teacher from Lebanon. "How dare they make such a mockery of one of our greatest heroes? Alad-din matters so much in the history of my people—it is an insult to let him appear on stage as if he is just an entertainment for children!"

You can imagine how stunned I felt by that outburst. (Just as well I hadn't mentioned that the 'Principal Boy' in pantomime is played by a girl, eh?). Bur how many more 'insults' might the Anglo-Celtic tradition unwittingly offer to migrants?

Mind you, I'd had my own fun earlier in the piece, when Adnan and Georges, also from Lebanon, expressed serious reservations about being taught by a woman, anyway! Very demeaning they seemed to find it.

"What are you doing here?" they asked me in the first week's lecture. "Why aren't you at home, looking after your husband as you ought to be?"

As the two-year period of our acquaintance wore on, we became better tuned to one another, I think. Maybe I just want to believe that, eh?

Caterina wasn't in the 1979 intake, but the first one in 1978.
She did brilliantly in it, and has since gone on to take a degree in Education while teaching full-time. Not only teaching Italian language and culture at her Primary school, but also at the Saturday school. Even though I didn't get the chance to lecture to that 1978 group, her reputation for excellence was such that a colleague of mine who **did**

teach them said to me in 1980: "Don't expect them all to be as good as Caterina, will you? She was one out of the box—very special."

At the time she came to us, having been a superb teacher in Italy, she was teaching Italian for Macquarie University on their Extra-Mural scheme. One of the classes was held in the evening, not far from my house. As Languages had always been one of my prime interests I decided to enrol with her. She was a terrific teacher, much helped by her husband who usually came along with her, taking part of the group for conversation. I got so involved that I had plans for going to Italy in one of the College vacations in 1981 to live with an Italian family and study in Perugia for a few weeks. Bad Luck! I can't have been meant to go, for all that I'd paid my deposit. My plans were somewhat disrupted by my getting run over while on the pedestrian crossing at Ross Street on Parramatta Road, necessitating a spell in Royal Prince Alfred Hospital and three months off work!

I must say Caterina didn't hold it against me, as we're still great friends. In fact, when I went to Sydney for the Reunion I stayed at her place.

Dearly-loved Overseas Teachers, I've never felt **more** bonded to any students I had. Thankyou all.

15. The Nurses' Communication Course

Before the Institute of Nurse Education was set up as an integral part of Sydney College of Advanced Education (the name agreed to by Sydney Teachers' College in 1975, or thereabouts) the English Dept. was asked to co-operate with Hospital Nurse Educators in the following way. Trainee nurses would continue to be instructed in the theory and practice of Ward Nursing within their own hospitals, (naturally! where else?) while coming in to the College to be taught Science and Communication. Each of the English lecturers involved had one or two groups of nurses to teach, some in the lecture rooms of the hospital, some in the College building on the University campus.

This was yet another three-year stint that was different, therefore intriguing. David, the colleague who had the responsibility of writing and organising this new course, had been trained to teach in Liverpool, England. So naturally we found we'd lots of ideas and methods in common! Of course all of us in the English Department had for years been teaching pupils in our Dip. Ed. and Dip. Teach. classes how to make themselves better understood in the classroom, whether in speech, body language or writing. With our nurses, all three modes of communication came into play just the same, but body language and speech took precedence over written work, although they had to acquire skill in writing patients' reports.

As you might expect, though, they'd all had much practice at school on the writing front: their needs now were in the areas of observing people closely, seeing how different people express themselves in their body language, and adapting their own style of body language to achieve better communication with their patients in the Ward.

We quoted and invented case-histories for them to discuss in pairs, in small groups, in the whole class, in essays. Many of our examples were of patients we knew or had heard of, who came from other countries, spoke other languages, and had very different health customs, beliefs and practices. How were our nurses to be sure they'd understood the needs of such patients? We had to include in the course considerable elements of ethnic and multi-cultural instruction, sensitisation and awareness before we could feel we'd done a good job. Not many hospitals in 1978-80 were routinely supplied with interpreters, or with teachers who not only knew but could also convey the special needs of migrant men and women.

Incidentally, as I've told some of my students, you didn't have to be **not** a native-English-speaker to find it impossible to make yourself understood by a young nurse! You may remember my telling you about the time in 1969 when I went into Gloucester House to have the first operation (an osteotomy) done on my arthritic hip. When I'd been returned from Theatre to my bed, no doubt groggy for some time, my first clear recollection is of a rather pretty, dark-haired nurse, aged about nineteen, coming into the room. She drew up the bed-trolley, placed on it the regulation wash-bowl, extricated my toilet bag from the bedside locker and went out of the room.

I lay there for a while, scared to sit up because of the pain in my thigh and hip, and totally convinced that the nurse would help me to sit up and wash when she returned from whatever duties had called her away. When she **did** come back, she looked at me somewhat unbelievingly as she asked "Aren't you going to wash yourself? Come on! Sit up!"

I did my best to lever myself up, feeling at least as unbelieving as she looked! What had led me to think that I'd be helped, just because I was a post-operative patient? Where was my pride? My ancient athleticism? Wherever those two had gone, I was now so much in pain that the tears began to pour. I looked at her, feeling ashamed of my helplessness, hoping for sympathy.

"What are you crying for?" she demanded.

"It hurts. I'm sorry. I can't cope with the pain now that I've tried to sit up," says I.

"You think **you're** in pain, do you?" She sounded so angry and exasperated.

"If **you'd** had a row with your boyfriend last night, as **I** did, and after he'd walked out on you you'd cried all night—well, then you'd know what real pain is."

I can't for the life of me remember what happened to my wash that morning—I fancy I wrung out my face-cloth in the water and wiped whatever of myself I could reach! What I **do** remember is having sundry counselling sessions with my nurse over the next couple of weeks, offering her an empathetic ear. I wonder if it would have helped or embarrassed her to know what a lecture-illustration that encounter became in the Nurses' Communication Course nearly ten years later?

Goodness! Here's another recollection from that 1969 stay in Gloucester House. The things that pop up once you open Memory's door. Things you didn't even record at the time, as far as you realised! Well, my children used to come across from Wesley College to see me after doing their homework and having tea, etc. They always wanted to know if there was anything they could bring across for me that I'd like to eat. (Don't we all do that when we've got members of the family or friends in hospital?). Egg custard was one delicacy I fancied. Another was Port Salut cheese, a treat we'd only recently discovered in one of those amazingly good delicatessens in Newtown. (There were all sorts of advantages to living for twelve years in Newtown—not least the Elizabethan Theatre before it got itself burnt down—but there was also the fun of seeing people's faces when you told them where you lived, before the Inner West was at all trendy!) Shut up, June, you've got off the point again.

Back to the Port Salut. After it was brought in, and what wasn't eaten right away was put into my cupboard, it had the most remarkable and unexpected effect. One that I only learned of after several days, from a slightly giggly nurse who asked me whether I'd noticed that the Sister-in-charge hadn't been in to see me for some time. I **had** noticed, vaguely, but had probably assumed it meant: a) she was exceptionally busy, b) she was entirely satisfied with the way her nurses were handling everything, or c) I was getting on so well that I didn't need any special supervision.

Not at all! The reason was that she couldn't stand the odour of Port Salut, and as long as there was any of it left in my cupboard she refused to come into the room! I can only hope that the smell departed on the same day that I did!

16. Graduate Primary teachers

One of the things that I noticed over the time of the Nurses' Communication Course was the number of men, especially graduates, who were choosing to go into Nursing as a profession. The same thing was happening in the field of Primary Teaching. Whereas it had been taken for granted until the early 70's that university graduates who elected to go into Teaching would certainly become High School teachers, we were now facing whole groups of graduates who wanted to be trained to teach Primary age kids.

So it was back to the drawing-board. We now had to design a course which in the space of one year would give enough School Practice to men and women who hadn't been in the atmosphere of a Primary school for at least ten years. It had always taken three years or more to achieve the training of our Dip. Teach. students, who came to us straight from High School, mostly only six years away from their own Primary schooling. In each of their years with us they would have the chance of seven or eight weeks of practical learning via School Practice. How were we going to give our Graduate Primary groups anything like the same amount of contact with their future constituents?

One of our innovations for them was to arrange a two-week period of observation and helping teachers in the schools before the College year started towards the end of February. For one or two of them that fortnight was enough to make them realise that Teaching was not the career for them.

I was exceptionally glad that I'd been able to learn so much about Primary work from that very first group, 108, I was given when I started lecturing in the College's English Department. Possibly even more so for the insights the Overseas Teachers had given me, because they were more recent.

The Dip. Ed. Primary sections were just as interesting as you'd expect. Some already had kids of their own, which was what had motivated them to want to get into the schools as teachers themselves. Some were incredibly artistic and/or musical, which gave them outright advantages when it came to thinking up and executing the most effective assignments. This showed out the most when I asked them to 'invent' solid, concrete aids to comprehension for any slower learners they might find in their classes. Some of the work they did for me took me right back to the first Primary classroom I saw in 1969, at Bourke Street Public School. The teacher had organised her Art and Craft lessons in order to transform the room into an underwater cave, complete with a mermaid's garden, and all done in crepe paper. Using that medium, it had been possible for the kids to create stunning lengths of seaweed, which waved about whenever people moved around the room!

The most rewarding occasions were taking my graduates to see demonstration lessons. Once, in particular, we went to see a Drama lesson at Haberfield Public, where they had a marvellously gifted teacher. She used the music of "Night on Bald Mountain", adapted from the original by Mussorgsky, to which her class improvised a dance-drama. It inspired many of my students to think of trying to use music for their drama lessons on School Practice.

Another bonus in originality came from one of the graduates who'd qualified in Architecture. He talked to us about the possibilities of transforming the 'standard classroom' by means of temporary partitions, thus facilitating group work, individual project work, and drama work of a more complex nature—e.g. setting up a 'village' with shops, tradesmen's workshops, households, fields, schools etc. Making the partitions could be done in his Art and Craft lessons, while measuring and costing the materials needed would give the class a period of doing number work with some purpose and relevance for their lives outside school, too.

Certainly any who'd opted for Primary teacher-training because they'd imagined it to be less tiring or less taxing than teaching in High School confessed before the year was out that working with energetic Primary-age kids took more out of them than they'd bargained for! Nobody regretted their choice enough to drop out, though.

17. Speakers' Workshop

All our Graduate classes had a weekly session of practice and instruction in 'How to Deliver Yourself Better in Teaching a Class'. Which sounds amazingly pompous, but boils down to "Speak up clearly and be interesting, or they'll go to sleep." (Sound familiar to anyone?). Over the years of thinking up, reading up, and pinching one's colleagues' bright ideas, activities and exercises for Speakers' Workshop tend to accumulate. Some of them worked well every year. Others were fruitful one year and fell flat the next. Here's a selection of them:

1) We usually had fun when each member of the class was asked to read something, using several different tones of voice. We read from a newspaper, an education text-book, favourite poems and prose pieces they brought in themselves, and hardest of all, the telephone book. Any of them would be easy enough to read aloud in one's normal style, maybe, but the exercise needed lots of grit when requested in front of your class-mates to produce a reading in one of the following styles of delivery: angrily, sleepily, seductively, boringly slowly, arrogantly, hesitatingly, uncomprehendingly, lovingly, dictatorially, pleasantly smiling.

I could, of course, use this exercise with almost any age or type of student—Primary, Secondary, Nurses or T.A.F.E. teachers in training, Physical Education students, Post-graduate Drama students an' all. It was especially useful when working at Yarrawood during College Camps in English, Drama and Special Education.

2) This second exercise was designed to encourage imaginative and convincing delivery of a tale that groups of three or four students had invented. I took in with me sundry objects collected from home, the more exotic or outrageous the better. They included a nutcracker of the type that uses a little marine wheel, turned by its handle to advance along a screw, compressing the nut, pincer-fashion, until the nutshell broke. There were mementoes collected on our journey out from England, interestingly-shaped pebbles, and my grandmother's ebony

dressing-table set including a hair-tidy, trinket-box, glove-stretcher and button-hook for fastening gaiters or long buttoned gloves. (You can imagine what glorious tales the students made up about **those** unfamiliar items!). Two objects in particular always elicited marvellous romantic stories: a carved sandalwood box, and an amber necklace dating back to 1922.

After the groups were formed and each given an object to discuss, the instructions were these: Decide what you want this object to represent. Which of the group is to be the owner or discoverer of it? Where did it come from? How much is it worth? Was it a native artefact that was originally stolen? (etc. etc.). Each member of the group is to tell a part of the story that you agree upon. The rest of us will judge how convincing, imaginative and well-told your story is.

The students would then take twenty minutes or so discussing the line they wanted to take. After that, the stories would be told by each group in turn, commented on and appreciated by the whole class. We usually needed a teabreak halfway through!

I always hoped that this exercise would create, enhance and increase the story-telling capacities of my students, giving them at least **one** extra method at their disposal for entrancing their future pupils!

Possibly my most lasting recollection from this particular exercise is of one young man from the group that had been given my mother's amber necklace round which to construct their story. His role in the telling was to pour cold water on any suggestion from the others that it was an ancient treasure from India, discovered during an archaeological expedition late in the previous century. (This was the group's chosen version). "Not at all!" said the student who'd been allotted the role of the sceptic. In his most scornful tone he added: "Anybody can see that this tale of an expedition find is a load of bullshit! It's a classic con. These beads are just a cheap trinket from Woolworth's, taken and hidden in the right place to be 'found' by the **one** member of the party who stood to make a great reputation and a load of money if this crazy tale caught on! Can't you all see that?

I'll pass the necklace round so's you can all see for yourselves what a cheap, mass-produced job it is!" So he did that. What a story-telling gift, eh? I can only hope he was able to make use of it when he had to teach Economics!

18. Body Language

That's enough of **that** variety of Exercises in Communicating. Let's have a look at another type that was evolved for the Nurses' Course—namely the language of body-movement and room-messages. I learnt a terrific amount about body-language from the opening lecture each half-year when the Nurse Education Communication Course began. David Spurgeon, who, you may remember my saying earlier, was in charge of this course, lectured to the whole group together, before the students were split up into seminar/lecture classes.

He asked if any of us had been at the airport when a large flight of Europeans or Asians had arrived, to be greeted by their waiting families? If so, did we remember how everybody had behaved? A fair summary of the answers offered to that question would be:

"Oh . . . laughing, screaming with joy, embracing one another, crying, kissing . . . . thoroughly embarrassing!" "Why embarrassing?" David asked.

"Because we were brought up to be reserved and controlled in public. Not to draw attention to ourselves by making a racket or jumping up and down like those people."

"How would your families ever know what you were feeling? Especially if they'd been waiting for you to come home from overseas for a long time?"

"Surely they could take it for granted that we were glad to be back, without all that hoo-hah?"

So now we'd been forced to take note of the considerable differences in 'usual behaviour' across a range of migrant cultures. How might those differences affect the way migrants approached health professionals in Australia? Nurses in particular needed to be aware of how they might be regarded in the hospital ward, remembering that not all countries or societies expect to be served in the same way when someone of their race or nation is sick in hospital. We wanted them to realise that non-verbal language might well be of greater significance in their attitudes and approaches to their patients, if they wanted to convey empathy and concern to those whose English understanding and fluency were hardly yet developed.

To work on this body language, and other aspects of the non-verbal, we worked out some intriguing 'acting out' exercises, which were lots of fun to perform. One of them I called 'The Threatening Advance'. Frowning uncharacteristically I would leave my table at the front of the lecture-room, walk swiftly towards one of the front-row students, pull up just in time, and pause. After a short time I asked "How does that make you feel?" Answers varied, but not much! "Scared!" "Worried and frightened." "Wondering what on earth I've done wrong this time!" "Have I offended her in some way without realising it?"

Then I would ask them when they'd last been in a similar situation, giving them the same sorts of feelings or reactions. Apart from possibly in schooldays, could they associate those reactions in any way with their hospital experience? More than one group responded to that question by recalling times when a doctor, senior Charge Nurse or Sister had swept into the ward unannounced, obviously not happy about something. Releasing laughter usually followed at this point, giving me the chance to ask them how **they** normally approached their bedfast patients.

So we next looked at the effects upon people that are created by different kinds of space around them. 'Intimate space'—practically touching, appropriate only to people on the most familiar, close terms; 'Personal space'—less close than 'Intimate', but still a distance within which you wouldn't want a stranger to intrude; 'Social space'—the accepted distance we keep from one another in our mixing at work, in the street, at parties or gatherings perhaps; 'Official space'—the most distant of all, belonging to our contact with others in an official capacity, at Union or Company or Annual Meetings.

Once we'd discussed these 'space' concepts, relating them as closely as we could to occasions arising in a nurse's work, we pulled out of our collective memories some familiar orders, and asked on what basis they stood and were 'obeyed'. "Go back to your place!" "Return to your seat!" "Kindly leave the room!".

These thoughts made some of the students remember how people commonly claim '**their** space' by placing a folder, a file, a briefcase (or once upon a time, even a hat!) on the seat they wish to occupy. Which again reminds me of how delighted they were when I told them of the famous retort from my part of the world: "Seats are kept by bums, not hats!"

As part of our examination of non-verbal communication, we looked hard at the 'messages' we get from rooms and buildings themselves. Those 'built environments', as the architectural fraternity calls them, included hospital wards, corridors, operating theatres and Nurses' Homes.

We could, and did, find immediate examples in the lecture room we were occupying at the time. If it was one of the familiar raked variety, with fixed bench-type desks all facing the front, where the lecturer's desk, table or lectern was to be found perched up on a dais and facing towards the students' desks, **what** is the message being conveyed to all and sundry? Isn't it "Here we have one learned person, who will tell all you others what to think and do. **Your** job in this room is to hear and believe, accept or repeat in assignments."?

I must say in passing, and not related to the Nurses, that lots of my trainee-teacher students got into bother on School Practice by imitating my style of teaching, perched on the front of my desk or walking about to emphasize my argument! (Sometimes the blood supply was quite cut off from my feet if I sat on the edge of the desk for too long, having as usual become absorbed in the discussion!)

Have you noticed how an atmosphere of Superior-to-Inferior is created if two people sit one on each side of a desk, facing one another, during an interview? If, however, they sit side by side, there isn't nearly the same feeling of "I am being interviewed. I must be on my best behaviour. I wouldn't want this person to assess me as I really am, would I?"

We acted out that situation too, reminding our nurses that they might very well one day be in the position of having to take case-history notes from their patients. If, then, they couldn't establish by means of body-language an aura of empathy, consideration and gentleness as well as competence and confidence, then they shouldn't expect to achieve truly honest information about the state of health of those patients. Especially so if they needed an interpreter, or if their culture required them to be accompanied by another member of their family. In that case even more loving care would be needed when organising the seating arrangements for such an interview!

As you can see, I recollect those Nurses' Communication classes from fifteen years ago with as much pleasure and fun as I do most of the other things I've told you about. Thank goodness I **have** been able to summon up **some** of the disasters, even if only one or two! Wonder where all the others hid themselves? Perhaps in a conveniently flattering memory-bank, eh?

19. A totally satisfying sideways move into Technical Teacher Education 1981-85

More than eight years have passed since I retired from lecturing in English after nearly twenty years at Sydney College of Advanced Education. My last four years there were even more fulfilling, if possible, than the previous fifteen had been—because I moved across from the College's Institutes for Primary and Secondary Education to it's Institute for Technical and Adult Teacher Education. As I was then 55, it seemed likely that T.A.F.E. teachers in training might just be more my bag, being nearer my age, and anyway more of a challenge!

At that time, February 1981, the College ran its Technical Teacher Education department in rented premises, comprising several floors of Gazal House in Wattle Street, Ultimo. This necessitated the use of an elderly lift, which is referred to in the work of one of my students that I'll include later in this chapter.

Did I say I thought they might be more my bag, at that age, than were my Primary and Secondary students? They turned out to be more than that! Exciting, challenging, satisfying, wonderfully happy-making— these would be much more fitting adjectives to describe them. It's high time I paid tribute publicly to those students, telling them again how terrific they were. Especially as I've found among 'June's Memorabilia' (carefully packed when moving house!) pieces of work they did for me that some of them never reclaimed—or forgot! They were so sure that they could **never** learn to express themselves in the way the College's 'Department of Communication' seemed to be going to ask of them! You'll see, as they did, later in the piece!

So many of them had left school and gone into Trade Apprenticeships because they didn't like school or hated their teachers—that's what they told me. **Now** here they were, having to train to **be** teachers. Just because they were such good tradesmen that they wanted to pass on to youngsters the skills they possessed. What you might call 'showing the kids what you can do best'.

Isn't that what every good teacher you ever had wanted to do? Me too! Why then do you suppose they suffered from such low self-esteem?

Butchers, brickies, cabinet makers, electricians, metal workers, automotive engineers and mechanics, computer experts and systems analysts, Real Estate men, teachers of Aeronautics, hairdressers, Art teachers, Home Economics teachers, Hospitality Industry people who taught at the Ryde Food School or the East Sydney Tech., teachers of Adult Literacy and Communication, Secretarial and Fashion aces . . . .

I even taught a gentleman who bore the illustrious title: 'The Last of the Australian Master-Plasterers'. Dear Raymond! His favourite author, if I remember rightly after twelve years, was Dickens. Can you beat it? And **still** they'd been conditioned to suppose themselves inferior to people like us, who had gone to college or university.

"Look!" I told 'em, "You can **all** do things that I can't, and never **will** be able to do!".

"But," they replied, "**you** can stand up in front of a class and **teach** them what you **do** know . . . and what's more, you learned all our names in the first week's lecture we had with you. Tell us how you do it, eh? That **would** be useful when we start with our new classes!"

So! All I had to do was to prove to them that they could express themselves in their own subjects at least as well as I could in mine. In Speaking **and** in Writing. I can't pass on to you their efforts in Oral English, or in Library Research and Assignment Writing, but I **can** give you some of their written work, can't I?

Early on in my time with them, to get them relaxed and beginning to believe they **were** going to enjoy what we were trying to achieve, I took in some 'Shape poems', in which the words are arranged in the shape of whatever object it is that you want to write about.

They chose their subjects to suit themselves, producing work on shapes as varied as a hammer, a draughtsman's table, a rail journey to Central, a small girl, a bottle, a football, a waterfall. I have included three of their efforts for you to see, on the following pages.

June Webb

river flowing down down
closer to the edge

right over the edge

water falling down down down down down

WATERFALL

POP
FIZZLE
GURGLE
guzzle
ABSTINENCE
PARTAKING
DRUNK
IT'S senseless empty

THE DRINKER

114

It was all just words, really, for forty years—wasn't it?

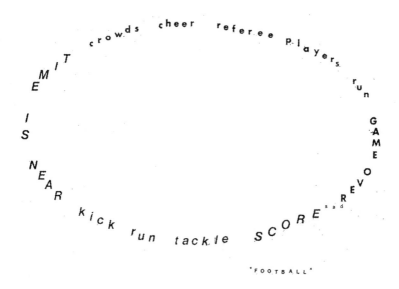

"FOOTBALL"

As the year wore on, some of them showed really special gifts for Writing that they **said** they never knew they had! In the Creative Writing periods and later at home, Patrick (a teacher of Foundry and Metal-work) produced the following two poems. 'Home-work' speaks for itself. 'Gazal' needs me to remind you perhaps of that ancient lift in the old premises. (Of course the young and strong could always run up the firestairs!). Another clue you may or may not need is to the meaning of Gazal's nick-name, as Patrick uses it in his verses. "The Mushroom Farm" or "The Old Mushroom" arose, as I'm sure lots of you will know, from an old student saying: "Keep 'em in the dark, and feed 'em bullshit!".

It was all just words, really, for forty years—wasn't it?

Home-Work

He sits upon his lofty perch,
Holds forth with dreaded rule;
The teacher hard must all survey
The pupils of his school.

We come to learn with shuffling gait,
Deep furrows on the brow;
No home-work done—hell, I'm late—
I'm sure to cop it now.

Full well know I what is in store,
Not having done my work;
Miscreant ears shall ring red-sore,
For home-work I did shirk.

Oh what a cruel existence
A student must endure—
An' I know that **'e'd** be better off
Without **me** 'ere, I'm sure.

'E'd be able to put 'is feet up,
An' **I** wouldn't 'ave ter wrack me brain—
'E wouldn't 'ave ter worry about me Mum
Every time I get the cane.

I better tell 'im **somefing**—
Like, I 'ad work to do—
An' me poor ol' Mum, she's bin real sick,
An' me Dad? Well, 'e shot through.

"Sir, I've worked me fingers to the bone
'Cos I 'ad to 'elp me mate,
So if I'd 'a stopped for 'ome-work, Sir,
I'd 'a got 'ere too darn late."

Yeah, ol' Sir 'e's a real good bloke,
I know 'e'll understand;
'E won't knock me block off
Or whack me on me 'and.

No, 'e's not goin' ter b'lieve that lot—
Oh 'eck, wot can I do?
The on'y thing I know of
Is to pack up and shoot through.

But a fella's got to be a man,
An' learn ter read an' write;
'E's got ter learn ter study 'ard
An' not jus' play an' fight.

So I'll face 'im square, an' own up true—
I'll accept me flamin' lot;
"My 'ome-work, Sir? You won't believe . . .
My 'ome-work? . . . . I forgot."

It was all just words, really, for forty years—wasn't it?

Gazal

There is a place, a learned place,
A place not known to all:
A Place rare loved, oft hated,
A place we call 'Gazal'.

For all who tread these hallowed halls,
These rooms of echoed fame,
They may forget some that ha' taught,
But ne'er that lustrous name.

To climb the winding staircase
To the knowledge high above,
Or ride 'the wild express' and pray
"Please God, do give it a shove!"

The rooms that ring with laughter,
And prose like "Back again!"
Or a piece that sounds like Lawson:
"A bloody bloke must be insane."

The grandeur of the Chalkboard,
The squeaks, the squawks, the dust;
The important Headings and the Build-up
And the Summary—all a "must".

All hail traumatic obso's,
Assignments and the like—
But none so fearful-minded
As deep-ended Ed. Psych.

"When you feel that you could choke 'em
Just give 'em a gentle pat,
And say 'That's a kindly fellow'
When you mean 'You rotten brat!'"

When you catch the big bloke in the corner
Carrying on like what the heck,
Just scold him gently, though it galls you,
Never 'wring his rotten neck.'

The intricacies of this ancient place
Seem far beyond our reach;
But with Learning, blessed Learning,
We'll sign "Yours truly and Dip. Teach."

All those who push on further
Can really knock 'em dead,
'Cause they'll no longer sign "Dip. Teach."
But "Yours truly and Dip. Ed."

Yet though this seat of Learning,
Sounding full of glee and gloom
Smelling of dust and polish,
Fondly called 'The Old Mushroom'

Will be but a distant memory
Of ages golden, past,
To untold men of wisdom—
But ones that will forever last.

We who came and learned here,
Who loved and hated it all,
In years from now will fondly recall
The rustic name 'Gazal'.

o–o–o–o–o–o–o–o–o–o–o–o–o

In October 1981 I managed to get myself knocked down while on a pedestrian crossing in Parramatta Road. (My Automotive students told people "June's been arguing with a truck!". They didn't know I was on foot, not in my car, at the time!). While I was in Royal Prince Alfred Hospital, recovering, one of them wrote the following poem. You won't be at all surprised to hear that it encouraged me a treat. For ages I showed it off fondly—I still think it's terrific! Reminds me sometimes of my Shelburne girls' approbation of my unshockability!

David's Appeal

Theory and Practice, Educational Psychology,
Assignments in late, so Student Apology—

This work is all right for all the young ladies,
But does not hold water with all us thick tradies.

Reading and Poetry and learning to spell—
We do all these things way down at Gazel.

For more happy students with Cognitives in tune
We need lots more teachers like our lady June.

Lunch-time around, down the Glasgow we go,
Two schooners of Old, and on with the show.

I don't want to worry you while in bed you lay,
But for these few words could you please give an 'A'?

For writing this verse your instruction did seed
The mechanical mind of Yours faithfully, D.Reed*

*Not his real name!

I've a feeling that set of couplets ought to be titled "Flattery Will Get You Anywhere!".

20. Final Musings

Heigh-ho! You can see why I loved them all, and missed them like hell when it was all over, can't you? Why **do** institutions (and Institutes!) insist that at the age of sixty their employees can no longer function properly? Considering that for the previous year those said employees have been delivering the absolutely ripe fruit of a lifetime's experience, don't you agree? I felt so useless and frustrated for a long time after 'retiring' (when all's said and done, nobody's ever called me The Retiring Type! Least of all my long-suffering students!) that I began to wonder if it wasn't all caused by the fact that I was missing my captive audience! All the most effective teachers of English Language and Literature are actors, aren't they?

Ha! My mind goes back to Miss Parker, who taught us Shakespeare's "The Tempest" in my Morecambe Grammar School days. She used to read the part of Caliban, the Monster, while members of the class acted out the other parts of Prospero, Miranda, Ferdinand, Stephano, Trinculo, and of course Ariel. Maybe Miss Parker was being thoughtful and complimentary to us, do you suppose, giving us the benefit of the doubt that we had **no** monsters in **our** class—so she alone would be capable of acting Caliban?

However that may be, we absolutely adored her for wrapping herself in her academic gown, stowing herself in the space under her desk, and growling, grumbling, sulking and pleading her way through the words of Caliban at the top of her powerful voice. Another of my as-yet-unsuspected role models?

I must say one of my most satisfying jobs of reading/acting occurred in 1970, when one of my Secondary Dip. Teach. groups was studying Shaw's "Pygmalion". None of them could work out how to read Eliza's part, as her Cockney dialect was printed more or less phonetically, to be read off the page exactly as it looked. (Reminds me of the advent of Strine, by Afferbeck Lauder—my students couldn't believe that text would make perfect sense if they'd only just **read aloud** what they saw on the page. You too?)

Back to Eliza Doolittle. It made me more giggly even than usual to see myself, a Lancashire girl, wading confidently into Shaw's representation of a broad Cockney mode of speech. Incidentally, when we arrived in Australia in January 1965 and started talking to the Sydney Uni. students, we were struck by how similar the Australian accent was to that of the Londoners with whom we'd been living and working for the previous fifteen months.

That classroom experience of mine of reading Eliza with as much power and flexibility as I could summon up, had two results. First, as was my hope, it gave my students the best chance of entering into the spirit and meaning of the play. Second, it led me to the realisation that Eliza's speech to Pickering, quoted at the beginning of my 'Slow Learner Opening Lecture', summarised for me, and still does, the road to learning, training, education in and for life's relationships and vicissitudes. So I'd like to repeat it finally as my Position Statement, as they say at those big International Conferences! (Does anybody ever take note of what the Others are 'Stating'? Or are they all preoccupied with how and when **they** are going to perform? Wondering how they'll impress the assembled multitude?)

Anyway, here goes.

"You see, really and truly, apart from the things anyone can pick up (the dressing and the proper way of speaking, and so on), the difference between a lady and a flower girl is not how she behaves, but how she's treated. I shall always be a flower girl to Professor Higgins, because he always treats me as a flower girl, and always will; but I know I can be a lady to you, because you always treat me as a lady, and always will."